THE
ROBERT B. PARKER
COMPANION

THE
ROBERT B.
PARKER
COMPANION

Dean James & Elizabeth Foxwell

BERKLEY PRIME CRIME, NEW YORK

THE BERKLEY PUBLISHING GROUP
Published by the Penguin Group
Penguin Group (USA) Inc.
375 Hudson Street, New York, New York 10014, USA
Penguin Group (Canada), 90 Eglinton Avenue East, Suite 700, Toronto, Ontario M4P 2Y3, Canada
(a division of Pearson Penguin Canada Inc.)
Penguin Books Ltd., 80 Strand, London WC2R 0RL, England
Penguin Group Ireland, 25 St. Stephen's Green, Dublin 2, Ireland (a division of Penguin Books Ltd.)
Penguin Group (Australia), 250 Camberwell Road, Camberwell, Victoria 3124, Australia
(a division of Pearson Australia Group Pty. Ltd.)
Penguin Books India Pvt. Ltd., 11 Community Centre, Panchsheel Park, New Delhi—110 017, India
Penguin Group (NZ), Cnr. Airborne and Rosedale Roads, Albany, Auckland 1310, New Zealand
(a division of Pearson New Zealand Ltd.)
Penguin Books (South Africa) (Pty.) Ltd., 24 Sturdee Avenue, Rosebank, Johannesburg 2196,
South Africa

Penguin Books Ltd., Registered Offices: 80 Strand, London WC2R 0RL, England

This book is an original publication of The Berkley Publishing Group.

Copyright © 2005 by Dean James and Elizabeth Foxwell.
Cover design by Annette Fiore.
Text design by Tiffany Estreicher.

The Edgar® name is a registered service mark of the Mystery Writers of America, Inc.

First edition: October 2005

Library of Congress Cataloging-in-Publication Data

James, Dean (Darryl Dean)
    The Robert B. Parker companion / Dean James and Elizabeth Foxwell.—Berkley trade pkb. ed.
       p. cm.
    Includes bibliographical references.
    ISBN 0-425-20554-1
    1. Parker, Robert B., 1932—Handbooks, manuals, etc. 2. Detective and mystery stories,
American—Handbooks, manuals, etc. 3. Randall, Sunny (Fictitious character)—Handbooks, manuals,
etc. 4. Stone, Jesse (Fictitious character)—Handbooks, manuals, etc. 5. Boston (Mass.)—In
literature—Handbooks, manuals, etc. 6. Spenser (Fictitious character)—Handbooks, manuals, etc.
7. Massachusetts—In literature—Handbooks, manuals, etc. I. Foxwell, Elizabeth. II. Title.

PS3566.A686Z74 2005
813'.54—dc22   2005048081

PRINTED IN THE UNITED STATES OF AMERICA

10   9   8   7   6   5   4   3   2   1

For Jean Swanson, dear friend and esteemed collaborator, from whom I have learned so much, sine qua non. *(DJ)*

For my sister, Margaret Foxwell, who gave me my first mystery novel and started me on this path, in love and gratitude for her unfailing support. (EF)

ACKNOWLEDGMENTS

From both of us: A special thanks to Robert B. Parker for his interest in, and support of, this project, and for writing the books that made it possible.

From Dean: First, thanks to Beth for working so hard and accomplishing so much in such a short period of time. Her organizational skills, efficiency, and professionalism are nothing short of amazing. As always, I offer huge thanks to our agent, Nancy Yost, and our editor at Berkley, Natalee Rosenstein, for their consummate professionalism and unflagging support. Sherry Virtz and Raylan Davis helped tremendously with obtaining reading copies of many of the books. My colleagues at Murder by the Book contributed their usual support and enthusiasm for all my writing projects. Finally, Tejas Englesmith continues to provide the support that only he can give, each and every day.

From Elizabeth: I'd like to thank my co-conspirator and pal Dean for asking me to participate in this project and for his never-flagging good humor and sense. I'd also like to thank our agent Nancy Yost and our editor Natalee Rosenstein for their advice and support. My colleagues at Heldref Publications also deserve a special thanks for their keen interest in all things mysterious.

CONTENTS

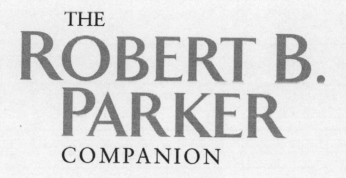

THE
ROBERT B.
PARKER
COMPANION

INTRODUCTION

Writing in an essay called "The Simple Art of Murder" in 1944, the immortal Raymond Chandler gave the world his conception of the private eye:

Down these mean streets a man must go who is not himself mean, who is neither tarnished nor afraid. . . . He must be a complete man and a common man and yet an unusual man. He must be . . . a man of honor, by instinct, by inevitability, without thought of it, and certainly without saying it. He must be the best man in his world and a good enough man for any world.

Unlike his predecessor (and former Pinkerton detective) Dashiell Hammett, who wrote convincingly of a world he himself had known, Raymond Chandler perhaps wrote of a world he wanted to be in, a world in which a man might move through the corruptions of the society around him, yet could manage to retain his own sense of honor while at the same time aiding those who needed the kind of help he could offer.

That, in a nutshell, is the American private eye, born of the violence and social changes of the United States in the 1920s. In the decades since then, the American private eye has become an icon of American popular culture, the loner who will fight to see justice done.

Many writers followed in the wake of Dashiell Hammett and Raymond Chandler, most notably Ross Macdonald, whose private eye hero Lew Archer becomes almost a surrogate parent for the abandoned children of all ages that he meets. In Archer, the private eye became more of a psychotherapist than an investigator, adding many nuances to Chandler's definition of the private eye.

Then, in 1974, came Robert B. Parker and a man called Spenser.

In creating Spenser, Parker followed in the tradition of his literary forebears: Hammett, Chandler, and Macdonald. Parker even wrote his Ph.D. dissertation on the subject of the private eye. But very quickly, Parker began to mold the icon into a character inimitably his own. A character, furthermore, who in the years since his first appearance has cast a long shadow on any writer of private-eye fiction.

From the wise-cracking loner who first appeared in *The Godwulf Manuscript* (1974), Spenser has grown and developed. He has built significant relationships—with Susan Silverman, Hawk, Paul Giacomin—and he remains a firm believer in adhering to his conception of honor. Early on in the series, he observes:

> I don't know if there is even a name for the system I've chosen, but it has to do with honor. And honor is behavior for its own reason. . . . Whatever the hell I am is based in part on not doing things I don't think I should do. Or don't want to do. (*Mortal Stakes*)

Spenser doesn't back away from violence, even while he sometimes questions the effect of so much violence in his life. In order to reassure him Susan Silverman tells him:

> "We all do what we need to, and what we have to, not what we ought to, or ought to have. You're a violent man. You wouldn't do

your work if you weren't. What makes you so attractive, among other things, is that your capacity for violence is never random, it is rarely self-indulgent, and you don't take it lightly. You make mistakes. But they are mistakes of judgment. They are not mistakes of the heart." (*Taming a Sea-Horse*)

Spenser doesn't indulge in violence purely for the sake of violence. He does nothing without purpose, without meaning in his own system of honor.

Spenser is obviously the kind of hero that readers can admire, because Robert B. Parker has long been a bestseller. With thirty-two Spenser novels (to date), neither Parker nor his most famous creation shows any signs of flagging. And, as if Parker hadn't accomplished enough already in a very distinguished career, he has created two other fascinating and appealing series characters, small-town cop Jesse Stone and female private eye Sunny Randall. That's not to mention, also, the nonseries novels: thrillers like *Wilderness* (1979) and *Double Play* (2004), westerns like *Gunman's Rhapsody* (2001) or a love story like *Love and Glory* (1983). Parker shifts from one type of novel to another with consummate ease, and, fortunately for his millions of fans, he continues to keep up this amazing productivity with two or three new books every year.

This book is intended, first, as a tribute to a writer who has helped redefine the modern crime novel in the last thirty years and who has long been a fixture on international bestseller lists. Second, it is a reader's guide designed to help readers search out particular information about their favorite Parker novels. For example, in which Spenser novel did Susan Silverman first appear? In which book did Spenser track down a terrorist group in Europe? Third, if you're one of those readers who has only recently discovered the joys of a novel by Robert B. Parker, this book will serve as an introduction to a rich body of work.

We invite you to join us in revisiting, if you're a longtime fan of Parker, or in discovering, if you're relatively new to his work, the world of Robert B. Parker.

Dean James and Elizabeth Foxwell

BIOGRAPHICAL INFORMATION

Robert Brown Parker was born in Springfield, Massachusetts, on September 17, 1932. He knew his future wife, Joan Hall, when they were both three, but it wasn't until they were both students at Colby College in Maine that they began dating. Parker graduated from Colby in 1954 with a B.A., and he and Joan Hall married in 1956. He went on to earn a Master's degree in English from Boston University in 1957, and a Ph.D. in 1971. His dissertation was a study of the fathers of the American private-eye novel: Dashiell Hammett, Raymond Chandler, and Ross Macdonald.

Parker served in the United States Army from 1954 to 1956 in Korea. From 1957 to 1959 he worked as a technical writer and group leader at Raytheon Company, then from 1959 to 1962 as a copywriter and editor for Prudential Insurance Company in Boston. During this time he also ran his own advertising business, the Parker Farman Company, from 1960–1962. At this point Dr. Parker reentered the academic world, becoming a teaching fellow and lecturer at Boston University while he pursued his Ph.D. He went on to teach at Massachusetts State College in Lowell, Suffolk University in Boston, and at Massachusetts

State College in Bridgewater. From 1968 until 1979, he taught at Northeastern University, becoming a full professor in 1977. He left the academic world in 1979 to write full time.

Robert and Joan Parker have two sons, David and Daniel. David, like the character Paul Giacomin, is a dancer and choreographer, while Daniel is an actor. Both David and Daniel are gay, and Dan has actually portrayed two of the gay characters (Spike and Detective Lee Farrell) from Parker's novels in television films. He also portrayed Father Ahearn in *Thin Air*.

During his long career Parker has received numerous awards. The first award was the prestigious Edgar Allan Poe Award for Best Novel, bestowed by the Mystery Writers of America; Parker earned it for the fourth Spenser novel, *Promised Land*. In 2002 the Mystery Writers of America named Parker Grand Master, an award given to writers who have compiled a significant body of work in the mystery genre. In addition, Parker was nominated for an Edgar for Best Episode in a TV Series for his work on *B. L. Stryker*. The Private Eye Writers of America have nominated Parker four times for their Best Novel Award, for *Early Autumn* (1982), *Ceremony* (1983), *The Widening Gyre* (1984), and *A Catskill Eagle* (1986).

As he enters his fourth decade as a novelist, and as one of America's favorite storytellers, Robert B. Parker shows little sign of slowing down. If anything, he is more productive than ever, now regularly producing two or three novels a year, all of which hit the bestseller lists. This amazing productivity is something for which his millions of fans around the world are truly grateful.

INTERVIEW WITH ROBERT B. PARKER

Question: Did you always want to be a writer? You had jobs which centered around the written word—advertising and academia. How did these experiences contribute to your eventual career path?

Answer: Yes, I always wanted to write. And in school I was always above average at it. The jobs I had were the result of the desire and proclivity, and were merely ways to support my family until I could write novels for a living. I think the Ph.D. in English, while it didn't teach me anything about writing, probably informed my imagination and maybe gave my writing what Chandler said Hammett lacked, "the sound of music from beyond the hill."

Queston: You read the classic detective stories in your youth, and your doctoral dissertation was on Chandler and Hammett. When Spenser first came to be, how influential were the classic models of the private eye?

Answer: The dissertation took me two weeks and did what it was supposed to do (get me tenure so I'd have time to write). But certainly when I began I was consciously trying to emulate Raymond Chandler.

Question: With Spenser you have very obviously diverged from the classic form of the private eye as a loner. Did you set out to do that from the beginning, or was it something that happened as the character evolved?

Answer: I am a happier man than Chandler was, and the center of my being is Joan and my sons. They are not only context. They are life. It was inevitable, I think, that I would evolve Spenser into a man with a similar center.

Question: One of the themes that seems to emerge consistently from the books is father-and-son relationships, e.g., Spenser's relationship with Paul Giacomin. This ties into a larger theme, responsibility for those who can't protect themselves. Would you say that this is perhaps Spenser's chief "operating principle"?

Answer: Spenser's operating principle is probably living life on his own terms, happily with Susan, as best he can. But obviously there is a knight-errant dimension about him, which Hawk's ferocious practicality balances off.

Question: Spenser's long and loving relationship with Susan Silverman is also markedly different from what we see in the classical form of the private-eye novel. Though they had some troubles in the early days, they now seem beyond that. Why did you make this relationship such a linchpin of the series?

Answer: Given that such a relationship is the linchpin of my life, I probably had little choice.

Question: In other interviews you have said that you don't worry about the plot, that you focus instead on character and the things you want to say in a book. Yet the plots are often complex and take quite a bit of detective work to unravel (e.g., in *Bad Business* or in *Paper Doll*). How much of the story do you know before you start the book? Does the book ever change as you write?

Answer: I begin only with a premise—i.e., in *Bad Business* Spenser investigates a corrupt corporation. Then I begin. I write ten pages a day. Chapter two grows out of chapter one, and chapter three grows out of chapter two, etc. I often don't know who did it until the book lays out and I may not know until nearly the end. Thus my writing and Spenser's investigation mimic each other. I may plan that a book will be about horse racing or baseball, but it always ends up being about the characters.

Question: In recent years you have published two and often three books a year. Can you tell us about your writing schedule and how you accomplish this?

Answer: I don't outline. Each weekday I write ten pages. I don't rewrite, I don't write a second draft. When I am finished, I don't reread it. Joan reads it to make sure I haven't committed a public disgrace, and, if I haven't, I send it in. Then I begin the next book. I am not obsessive about this, if there are things that interfere occasionally, in which case I may not write some Tuesday. When I have finished my ten pages—which usually takes from about eight AM to two PM, I work out. I spend three days a week doing Pilates training, I climb twelve flights of stairs two days a week, and take a two-mile walk one day.

Question: A few years ago you started two new series, the Jesse Stone books and the Sunny Randall books. Where did the new series sleuths come from? What different issues can you explore that separate these books from the Spenser novels?

Answer: Some years ago Joan and I decided to no longer hustle Hollywood, and I noticed that writing a Spenser novel took about two months. I invented Jesse Stone so I could try my hand at a third person narration, and a guy who was nowhere near as evolved as Spenser. Jesse has problems with alcohol and his ex-wife. Spenser is complete, Jesse is a life work in progress. I also liked writing about a cop and a small-town police force. Sunny Randall was invented at the behest of Helen Hunt, who wanted me to invent someone for her to play in a series of movies. We agreed that I would write a novel. Putnam would publish. Sony would buy it for Helen, and Helen would star. Everything worked fine up to actually making the movie. That is in limbo (nothing ever dies in Hollywood, though the birth rate is also low). Sunny did well and my publisher urged me to continue, so I did. I lean heavily on Joan for the woman's point of view here. And I am able to write about things from the perspective of someone of great courage but limited physical strength.

Question: It has long been evident that you're a baseball fan, and in *Double Play* you wrote a novel that is both a tribute to Jackie Robinson and an exploration of racial attitudes. It's also somewhat autobiographical, through the voice of Bobby. What was the genesis of this book? Will we ever see the main character, Burke, again? Or get any more of Bobby's story?

Answer: The genesis was simply that I wanted to write it. We pitched it around Los Angeles as a movie idea, without success, and, because I wanted to say something about a great man, I turned the idea into a novel. As for seeing Burke, or Bobby, again—I don't know. I have no master plan.

Question: In the most recent Spenser novel, *Cold Service*, Hawk is seriously injured after failing to protect a client. After having Hawk seem invincible for so many years, why did it happen now? It certainly provides some interesting insights into the character.

Answer: I think you answered your own question. I wanted to explore more of Hawk, which I can only do through Spenser's point of view, and I am glad if you got some insights.

Question: The relationship between Spenser and Hawk is just as important as that between Spenser and Susan, in many ways. Was this something you ever expected when you first introduced Hawk?

Answer: Hawk began as just another worthy opponent in *Promised Land*, but in the next book, *Judas Goat*, when I needed someone to back up Spenser, Hawk seemed a logical choice and away we went. He is, racial pun intended, kind of Spenser's dark side. And he gives me an opportunity to do my small riff on race relations.

Question: There has been a TV series, *Spenser: For Hire*, as well as TV movies featuring Spenser. How involved in these were you? Were you happy with the way they turned out? Will we see any more of Spenser on the screen? Or any of the other characters, like Jesse Stone or Sunny Randall?

Answer: I was theoretically a consultant on *Spenser: For Hire* but in fact contributed little. I had a large role in three movies we did for A&E starring Joe Mantegna. In neither case did I think the movies got it right (including the ones in which I had a large role). The reasons would make a book, but the problem is not talent, so much as money. Which is the nature of Hollywood. On February 20, 2005, Tom Selleck will star as Jesse Stone in *Stone Cold* on CBS. My contributions to that have been modest.

Question: Finally, is there any special message you would like to send to your multitude of fans who might be reading this book?

Answer: Thanks for your support.

THE SPENSER NOVELS

With the publication of *Cold Service* (Putnam, 2005), Robert B. Parker has published thirty-two novels about Spenser. We have summarized the plot of each novel in this section. For more information, read (or reread) the series!

The Godwulf Manuscript (1974)

A priceless illuminated manuscript from the fourteenth century is stolen from a Boston university library. Suspected in the theft is SCACE (Student Committee Against Capitalist Exploitation), a radical campus group. The university president hires smart-aleck PI Spenser to recover the manuscript. Spenser talks to SCACE secretary Terry Orchard and meets Terry's mean, possessive boyfriend Dennis Powell, a SCACE official and sometime drug dealer. Later, Spenser is called to Terry's apartment and finds a stoned Terry and a very dead Dennis. Terry claims that she was set up, and her wealthy parents hire Spenser to clear her of the murder charge. During the course of his investigation, Spenser encounters Joe Broz, a crime boss with more than a passing interest in a missing document; Mark Tabor, SCACE's political counselor who knows more than he's telling; Lowell Hayden, an English professor with a secret life; Judy Hayden, his close-mouthed wife; Iris Milford, a campus journalist; Brenda Loring, a nubile university secretary; and Terry's dead former roommate Catherine Connelly. Terry disappears into the dubious embrace of a local cult, forcing Spenser to rescue her. The manuscript reappears, and Spenser is pressured to drop the matter and allow Terry to be convicted. He is nearly killed in facing down the multiple murderer and discovers that there is much more to the case than simple theft.

God Save the Child (1974)

Smithfield residents Roger and Margery Bartlett hire Spenser to find their missing teenage son Kevin, with whom they have a troubled relationship. After delivery of a ransom demand and discussions with Lieutenant Healy, the able state police investigator, and the town's lesser-qualified Chief Trask, Spenser works undercover at a riding stable in an effort to trap the kidnappers, but he is not successful. A hearse with a dummy body proves to be a false clue. Spenser visits Kevin's guidance counselor, Susan Silverman, who provides a lead to a commune run by a former bodybuilder, Vic Harroway. Margery Bartlett's life is threatened, and Spenser finds the body of Earl Maguire, the Bartletts' attorney, at the Bartlett residence. Spenser discovers that Kevin has a history with Harroway, Harroway's commune is actually a brothel, and Ray Croft, the Bartletts' doctor, is involved in the operation. Spenser and Susan get cozy. Spenser has a showdown with Harroway, reuniting Kevin with his parents, and finds Croft dead. This final discovery leads to an unexpected twist in the case.

Mortal Stakes (1975)

An executive with the Boston Red Sox, Harold Erskine, calls Spenser in to investigate pitcher Marty Rabb, who may be fixing games. As a cover, Spenser pretends to be a writer working on a book on baseball, and in this guise he approaches Rabb and others associated with the Sox organization. Jack Little, who handles PR for the Sox, assists Spenser with information on the players and the organization. Quick to catch Spenser's interest is the Sox's flamboyant announcer, Bucky Maynard. Little warns Spenser not to mess around with Maynard, who can easily destroy the reputation of anyone who crosses him. Accompanying Maynard everywhere he goes is Lester Floyd, a young man with a quick fuse, and Spenser has little trouble igniting it.

As Spenser begins digging into Rabb's history to discover what, if anything, might lead the talented athlete to fix games, he begins to zero in on Rabb's wife, Linda. The more he investigates Linda, the more questions Spenser finds. Convinced the case hinges on Linda's past, Spenser travels to the small town of Redford, Illinois. From there, the trail leads him to New York City and ultimately back to Boston. Spenser comes up with a plan to save Marty Rabb and his family, and though the plan will force Spenser to make some tough moral choices, he doesn't shrink from the challenge.

Promised Land (1976)

Hyannis real-estate developer Harv Shepard hires Spenser to find his wife Pam, who has disappeared. Spenser learns that Pam has a reputation for sleeping around and locates her in New Bedford, where she has been staying with a pair of radical feminists. Pam tells Spenser that her husband is smothering her and that she does not know if she can return to him. In the meantime, Spenser discovers that Shepard cannot repay a hefty loan from the local loanshark, King Powers, and has been beaten by Powers's hired gunman, Hawk. To finance their violent women's movement, Pam's friends rob a bank and kill the security guard, thus involving Pam in murder. Spenser works to implicate Powers in a gun sale to the radical feminists and thus extricate the Shepards from their dangerous situation, nail Pam's friends for the guard's murder, and put Powers behind bars. The Shepards' marital troubles lead Spenser and Susan Silverman to discuss their commitment to each other.

The title *Promised Land* refers to both Harv Shepard's floundering real estate company and Cape Cod, the setting for the book.

The Judas Goat (1978)

Wealthy businessman Hugh Dixon summons Spenser to his home in Weston to discuss a job. Dixon, his wife, and their two daughters were victims of a bomb in London the previous year. Dixon survived, though he was permanently disabled; his wife and daughters were killed. Now Dixon wants Spenser to find the group responsible for the bombing and see that they pay. He doesn't care whether Spenser kills them or catches them and turns them over to the police. He'll pay Spenser a bounty for each one caught or killed. The group considered responsible calls itself "Liberty," and there are nine members, eight men and one woman. Spenser heads to London and baits a trap, hoping to flush Liberty out in the open. He hopes that one of the members of the group will play "judas goat" and lead him to the rest.

The group makes several attempts on Spenser's life, and he calls in Hawk to join him as back-up. Together Spenser and Hawk follow the trail from London to Copenhagen to Amsterdam and, finally, to Montreal during the 1976 Olympic Games. Spenser and Hawk flush out the remaining members of the group and put an end to a monstrous plot that would disrupt the Olympic Games.

Looking for Rachel Wallace (1980)

Publishing executive John Ticknor hires Spenser to protect lesbian author Rachel Wallace, who has written a controversial book, *Tyranny*, about discrimination against gay women and is receiving threatening letters and phone calls. There is an attempt to hit Wallace with a cream pie at a book signing, and two cars try to run Spenser's car off the road. Wallace sleeps with Julie Wells, a model, while a discomfited Spenser lurks outside. Wallace fires Spenser after he punches both an obnoxious protester blocking a library entrance and security officials at an insurance agency. Shortly thereafter, Wallace is kidnapped. Spenser discovers that the library protester is Wells's brother Lawrence Turnbull English, Jr., who has ties to right-wing groups, including one that claims to have kidnapped Wallace. Members of one of the groups beat up Spenser, and he discovers that the English family blames Wallace for Wells's homosexuality. Spenser enters English's house on a pretext, finds Rachel confined in the attic, and kills English and a henchman in self-defense. Although Wallace is grateful to Spenser for her rescue, she still disapproves of his code as a PI.

Early Autumn (1981)

Patty Giacomin walks into Spenser's office, wanting to hire him to find her fifteen-year-old son, Paul. Mrs. Giacomin claims her ex-husband, Mel, Paul's father, has taken the boy out of spite, because the court awarded her custody. Spenser takes the case, very quickly finds Paul, and returns him to his mother. Spenser observes that Paul appears underweight for his age, is interested only in watching television, and seems to be little more than a pawn in a power struggle between his parents.

When Mel Giacomin attempts to take Paul by brute force, using hired muscle, Spenser saves the day. By now Spenser's compassion has reluctantly been aroused, and he decides to do something to "save"

Paul from his parents. He wants to teach Paul how to rely on himself, since he obviously cannot rely on either of his parents to take care of him the way they should. Spenser and Paul head off for the Maine woods, where they begin building a cabin on land Susan Silverman received in her divorce settlement. Paul at first is reluctant and resentful, but Spenser wins him over, and by the end of the book, he is strong enough to stand up for himself. But to keep Paul's parents from mucking up his life any further, Spenser has to spike their guns, and so he does.

A Savage Place (1981)

Spenser, referred by past client Rachel Wallace (*Looking for Rachel Wallace*), travels to Los Angeles to protect KNBS-TV reporter Candy Sloan. Sloan, who has uncovered payola and a possible mob connection to the film industry, is beaten up. Spenser discovers that her sometime boyfriend and stuntman Mickey Rafferty witnessed a payoff from producer Sam Felton to a mob underling. Sloan and Spenser interview Roger Hammond, head of Summit Studios, which employs Felton; Hammond denies involvement with the mob. Sloan and Spenser sleep together. They visit Peter Brewster of Oceania Industries, Hammond's boss, who also denies a Mob connection. Rafferty is shot to death. Sloan and Spenser interview Felton, who denies killing Rafferty; Spenser shoots one of Felton's henchmen in self-defense. Sloan sleeps with Brewster in an attempt to get information. Felton turns up dead. Spenser discovers the body of Sloan, who has been shot. He storms Oceania Industries and forces Brewster to confess on camera to Sloan's murder. Despite pending charges against him, Spenser is permitted to return to Boston by the detective in charge of the case.

Ceremony (1982)

Worried about one of her students who seems to have disappeared, Susan Silverman brings Spenser to talk to the parents, Harry and Bunni

Kyle. Harry doesn't want his daughter April back, calling her "a goddamned whore" in the novel's memorable opening line. But Bunni Kyle is worried for her daughter, and Spenser takes the case for a dollar retainer from her. Harry Kyle had seen April tricking in Boston's notorious Combat Zone, and Spenser heads there to begin tracking her down. An encounter with a black pimp, Trumps, and one of his women clues Spenser in to the fact that there is something odd about April Kyle. After that, Spenser, with Hawk at his side, confronts another pimp, Red, for whom April had been working.

By persevering, Spenser makes it through the maze of deception surrounding April's whereabouts and locates her, only to lose her again. Determined now to find the girl and to save her from a bad situation, Spenser continues to work with Hawk and Susan. One of Susan's colleagues in education, Mitchell Poitras, has a very suspicious link to April and other runaway teens and to pornography. In the end, Spenser has to decide how best to "save" April Kyle, and his answer to the dilemma is a haunting one.

The Widening Gyre (1983)

Spenser signs on as head of security for born-again senatorial candidate Meade Alexander. Some young campaign volunteers are roughed up, and Spenser knocks out the thugs responsible. The incident leads Alexander to tell Spenser that he has received a videotape of his wife having sex with a college student. Spenser suspects that the blackmail attempt comes from Congressman Robert Browne, Alexander's opponent who is tied to Boston mobster Joe Broz. When Spenser confronts him, Browne denies any involvement and threatens Spenser. Spenser reunites with Susan Silverman in Washington, D.C., and tracks down the location where the videotape was filmed: the apartment of Gerry Broz, Joe's son. Further investigation reveals that Gerry Broz is dealing in drugs and hosting "granny parties" in which older women and young men have intercourse and are secretly filmed. Spenser takes this information to Broz Sr., who claims to be unaware of his son's activities. Spenser is shot by two of Broz's henchmen and kills them. Hawk accompanies Spenser to a meeting with Broz in which they come to an uneasy truce. Broz will give the videotape to Spenser, and Spenser will not tell the newspapers about Gerry Broz. Alexander is not expected to be elected.

Valediction (1984)

Spenser attends Susan Silverman's graduation at Harvard—Susan has finally attained her Ph.D.—and shortly afterwards, at the "victory celebration," Susan drops a bombshell. After being in Washington, D.C., for a year on an internship, she's moving to San Francisco to take a job there. Stunned, bereft, Spenser seems unable to cope, until his surrogate son, Paul Giacomin, comes home for the summer. Paul has taken a job with a small dance company, and the owner and director of the company, Tommy Banks, hires Spenser to find one of his dancers, Sherry Spellman. She is Banks's girlfriend, and he claims she was abducted by a religious group, the Reorganized Church of the Redemption. Sherry had once been a member of the group, and Banks wants Spenser to find her and free her from them.

Spenser agrees to find Sherry and try to talk to her, to determine whether she is with the group of her own free will. He talks to the head of the group, Bullard Winston, who agrees to let Spenser talk to her. Sherry seemingly is happy to be with the group again, away from the possessive Tommy Banks, but Spenser is intrigued by the setup of the organization. He continues to monitor them, keeping an eye on Sherry, and the further he digs into the group and its finances, the more he is convinced there is something very shady going on. As he tries to handle his emotional response to Susan's leaving him, Spenser has to decide who is the villain and who is the victim in a very convoluted case.

A Catskill Eagle (1985)

Susan writes Spenser that Hawk has been arrested in Mill River, California. Hawk is charged with killing a security consultant for Russell Costigan, Susan's boyfriend, and assaulting several police officers. Hawk claims he was set up. Spenser conceals a gun in a fake cast and breaks Hawk out of jail. They hide out in San Francisco, and Spenser learns from Hawk and Susan's psychiatrist that Susan cannot choose between Russell and Spenser and may be held against her will. In search of Susan, Spenser and Hawk storm the home of Jerry Costigan, Russell's father and a dangerous arms merchant, and later burn down his lodge in Washington. Lieutenant Martin Quirk negotiates a deal with the FBI and the CIA in which the charges will be dropped against Spenser and Hawk in exchange for killing Jerry. Spenser and Hawk infiltrate Jerry's mercenary training camp, foment an uprising, and snatch Susan from Russell in the confusion. Hawk and Spenser foil a subsequent attempt by Jerry to kill them. With Russell's assistance, Spenser finds Jerry in Idaho and shoots him, and, because of a promise to Susan, leaves Russell alone. Susan chooses to stay with Spenser.

Taming a Sea-Horse (1986)

Patricia Utley, the high-class madam Spenser first met in *Ceremony* (1982), summons him to New York to talk to April Kyle, who has walked out on her job. One of Ms. Utley's staff has traced April to another call house, and according to Ms. Utley, April will eventually be traded off to somewhere less plush. The downward spiral will continue, unless Spenser once again manages to get to April and bring her back. April agrees to meet Spenser, and she tells him that she's working at the new establishment to earn money to help her boyfriend, a black musician named Robert Rambeaux, who's enrolled at Juilliard. Spenser quickly determines that while Rambeaux is a musician and is indeed enrolled at Juilliard, he's also a pimp. A conversation with one of Rambeaux's whores leads Spenser more deeply into a deadly maze of corruption and murder.

When April Kyle once again disappears and Rambeaux is murdered, Spenser follows a path that eventually takes him to the Caribbean; Portland, Maine; and back to Boston and the exclusive Crown Prince Club. Big money is at stake, not to mention the reputations of some of Boston's wealthiest and most prestigious men. Spenser braves it all for the sake of April Kyle.

Pale Kings and Princes (1987)

Garrett Kingsley, wealthy owner and editor of the *Central Argus*, hires Spenser to investigate the murder of his reporter Eric Valdez, who was nosing into Wheaton's drug trade and has a reputation as a ladies' man. In Wheaton, Spenser encounters stonewalling and threats by townspeople, local cops, police chief Bailey Rogers, and produce businessman Felipe Esteva, who employs Rogers's son Brett as a driver. Thugs threaten Spenser and burn his car; he wounds one of them. Rogers is shot to death. Brett threatens Spenser with a gun given to him by Esteva. Spenser takes it and learns from Massachusetts state trooper Lundquist that it was the gun that killed Rogers. When Brett drives an Esteva-owned tractor trailer to Maine and picks up a shipment of mackerel, Spenser hijacks it and discovers nearly three hundred kilos of cocaine under the fish. Spenser later finds Brett dead. He learns that Rogers was sleeping with Esteva's wife. Hawk, Spenser, and Lundquist shoot it out with the individuals involved in the cocaine shipment.

Crimson Joy (1988)

A serial murderer, dubbed the "Red Rose Killer" by the press, is on the loose in Boston, and the cops call in Spenser to help. The reason: The killer could be one of their own, and Martin Quirk needs someone he can trust. The killer has earned his sobriquet because he leaves a long-stemmed red rose with each of his victims. The victims are African-American, and the police also fear that racial tensions in Boston could ignite if they don't find the killer quickly enough.

Spenser, working with Hawk as well as the police, begins to make some headway. The killer, however, seems always to remain at least one step ahead. Then comes the terrifying moment when the killer leaves a rose for Susan Silverman. Spenser and Hawk are more determined than ever to get the killer before he can harm Susan, but it's just possible that the murderer is one of Susan's own clients. Because of her professional ethics, Susan can't say which of her clients she thinks is possibly the killer. Spenser is stymied briefly, but in the end, he gets his man, as always.

Playmates (1989)

Spenser is hired to investigate allegations of point shaving in Taft University basketball games. Coach Dixie Dunham denies the charge and warns Spenser away from his players. Dwayne Woodcock, the star forward for the team, also denies the allegation. Spenser's friend and former Celtics player Tommy Christopher views game tapes and confirms that Woodcock and possibly guard Danny Davis are involved in point shaving. Spenser confronts Woodcock, discovers that Woodcock is illiterate, and tells Dunham about Woodcock's activities. Dunham benches Woodcock. Bobby Deegan, a Brooklyn "wiseguy" behind the point shaving, attempts unsuccessfully to bribe Spenser, tries to hire Hawk to kill Spenser, and pays hitmen to shoot Spenser, a plot that is foiled by Spenser and Hawk. University president Adrian Cort fires Spenser when Spenser, protecting Woodcock for the sake of Woodcock's classy girlfriend, refuses to report on the case. Deegan has Davis murdered and attempts to kill Woodcock, but is thwarted by Hawk. In return for Deegan's testimony in a New York robbery case and Woodcock's promise to learn to read, Spenser engineers a deal for Deegan that will end the point shaving and secure a future for Woodcock.

Stardust (1990)

Susan Silverman is acting as technical advisor for a television program being filmed in Boston, a show featuring a psychiatrist, Dr. Shannon Cassidy. Susan brings Spenser onto the set because the series's volatile star, prominent television actress Jill Joyce, claims she's being stalked. At turns seductive and abusive, Jill refuses to give Spenser much concrete information on which to base her claims of being harassed. Spenser realizes that Jill, while she's a total mess psychologically, is terrified, and he is determined to find out why. The situation turns deadly when Jill's body double, Babe Loftus, is found murdered.

Seeking answers in Jill Joyce's past, Spenser starts digging. A former lover of Jill's, powerful businessman Stanley Rojack, asserts that Jill asked for his help in scaring off a man named Wilfred Pomeroy. Spenser easily tracks down Pomeroy, who confesses that he was once married to Jill. He met her in San Diego, and Spenser heads to California to find more answers. He crosses paths with a powerful Hispanic crime boss, Victor del Rio, who once had a relationship—and a daughter—with Jill, and he meets Jill's estranged parents. Long divorced, neither of them has had much contact with their daughter.

Complications continue to arise, but eventually Spenser finds the one secret in Jill's past that lies at the heart of the present situation. And, in a finale reminiscent of *Early Autumn*, Spenser takes Jill to Susan Silverman's cabin in Maine for his own special brand of therapy.

Pastime (1991)

As the book opens, Susan Silverman introduces Spenser to Vigilant Virgin, a solid chocolate German shorthair pointer, "three years old and smallish for her breed." Susan's ex-husband (colorfully nicknamed "Boink Brain" by Spenser) owns the dog, but he's moving to England and has given the dog to Susan. Though at first he puts up a show of resistance, Spenser quickly succumbs and christens the dog with a new name, Pearl. As it turns out, Spenser in his youth had a similar dog named Pearl, and in this book, Spenser tells Susan more about his childhood and youth than he has ever been willing to before.

In keeping perhaps with the theme of revisiting the past in this book, and of the ongoing conflicts between parent and child, Paul Giacomin returns. Now nearly twenty-five, Paul asks Spenser to help him find his mother, Patty, who has disappeared. Patty has never been a particularly nurturing mother, but Paul is naturally worried. He and Spenser set out on the trail, and eventually they find her in hiding with a new boyfriend, Rich Beaumont.

Beaumont has run afoul of Gerry Broz, son of Boston crime kingpin Joe Broz, and he's doing his best to keep from getting himself killed, with Patty more or less willingly by his side. Gerry, inept and unstable, is angered over Spenser's intervention in the situation, and Gerry's actions pose a question of loyalty for his father and his father's longtime lieutenant, Vinnie Morris. There are no easy answers in this story about family loyalties, but through it all, Spenser's care for his "adopted" son shines warmly.

Double Deuce (1992)

Spenser and Susan move in together. After a fourteen-year-old girl and her baby are killed in a drive-by shooting, Hawk and Spenser team up to remove the gangs around Double Deuce, a Boston housing project. Joining them is Hawk's girlfriend, Jackie Raines, a television producer, who plans to do a program on the gangs. They stake out the Hobart Street Raiders, led by the twenty-year-old Major Johnson, and Hawk decks a gang member. Hawk and Spenser discover that the Hobarts are dealing drugs for Tony Marcus, a local black crime boss. Spenser learns that the murdered girl's boyfriend is a rival gang member named Tallboy, who is subsequently killed by Johnson. One of the Hobarts grabs Raines; Hawk disarms him with one shot. Spenser and Hawk arrange with Marcus to move his drug operation and the Hobarts from Double

Deuce. They discover that Marcus's bodyguard killed the teenager and her baby as a way of enforcing Marcus's authority, and they trap Marcus into admitting the crime on tape. Quirk and Belson arrest Marcus, and Johnson agrees to testify against him. Susan and Spenser find that living together is not for them, and Spenser moves out.

Paper Doll (1993)

Olivia Nelson was brutally murdered one evening near her home in an exclusive Boston neighborhood, and her husband, Loudon Tripp, has hired Spenser to find the killer. The police have made very little progress on the case, partly because the dead woman seems to have had no enemies and also because they have been unable to find a motive for her death. Is it truly just a random killing? Spenser talks to the homicide detective assigned to the case, Lee Farrell, and Farrell tells him, with some bitterness, that he has been given a number of hopeless cases. Farrell is openly gay, and he believes he is given such cases because of this.

Spenser decides that he must seek answers to Olivia Nelson's death in her past. Accordingly, he travels to Alton, South Carolina, where she was born, to try to dig up information. There, to his surprise, he discovers that Olivia's father, "Jumper" Jack Nelson, a notorious womanizer, is still living, though Olivia had told her husband he was dead. Nelson claims that his daughter is married to a black man from Africa and is living there with her husband. Spenser spots a photograph of a young woman who looks very much like Olivia Nelson, and soon he begins to wonder: Who was the murdered woman?

Someone, however, wants Spenser to mind his own business, and he winds up in jail in Alton, and only a timely intervention from Quirk keeps Spenser from getting worked over. Who is so anxious to stop the investigation? And why? The answers to these questions lead Spenser to the very dark secrets at the heart of the Tripp and Nelson families and to some surprising revelations.

Walking Shadow (1994)

Port City Theater Company actor Craig Sampson is shot dead while on stage. Spenser, in the audience with Susan, encounters Port City police chief DeSpain. He learns that someone is following artistic director Demetrius Christopholous and actress Jocelyn Colby. Spencer is threatened by restaurateur Lonnie Wu, husband of company board member Ricki Wu and brother-in-law of the head of Chinese organized crime in the area. Wu also is smuggling illegal immigrants into the country. Spenser nabs a member of an Asian street gang outside of his apartment, and he and Hawk dodge a drive-by shooting in Port City. Spenser enlists former Joe Broz employee Vinnie Morris as backup and Harvard student Mei Lingas as translator. Hawk and Morris foil another attempt on Spenser's life. Spenser learns that Ricki Wu and Sampson were involved and that Colby invented the stalker story and followed Christopholous. Spenser receives a videotape that shows a bound and gagged Colby. Lonnie Wu is found beaten to death. Spenser discovers that Wu's men killed Sampson in retaliation for the affair and that DeSpain had an affair with Jocelyn that wrecked his marriage and career. He also learns that Colby faked her kidnapping and that DeSpain killed Wu, believing that Wu kidnapped Colby. Morris shoots DeSpain while he is attempting to escape.

Thin Air (1995)

Frank Belson's young second wife, Lisa St. Claire, has disappeared, and Belson seeks out Spenser at Henry Cimoli's Harbor Health Club to ask about the time Susan Silverman left Spenser. At first Belson doesn't want any help looking for his missing wife, but when an attempt is made on his life and he's seriously injured, it's time for Spenser to step up to the plate. Searching for answers in Lisa St. Claire's past, Spenser discovers that the young woman was not everything she claimed to be. The investigation leads Spenser to Lisa's divorced parents, neither of whom has much of a connection to the troubled young woman. The trail takes Spenser to Los Angeles and then back again to the Boston area.

Lisa's former lover, a handsome, volatile young man named Luis Deleon, has kidnapped Lisa, and scenes from Lisa's point of view are interspersed throughout the book. Deleon is engaged in a turf war in Proctor with crime boss Freddie Santiago, and Santiago lets it be known he'll be only too glad if someone takes Deleon out of the picture for him. With Hawk away in Burma, Spenser needs backup, and he calls on Chollo, muscle for L.A. crime boss Victor del Rio. Together Spenser and Chollo face down Deleon in order to bring Lisa St. Claire safely home to her husband.

Chance (1996)

Boston crime boss Julius Ventura hires Spenser to find his missing son-in-law Anthony Meeker. Spenser suspects that Ventura is motivated by more than concern for his daughter Shirley. Meeker was Ventura's bag-man between him and rival bosses Gino Fish and Fast Eddie Lee and could have skimmed from them. Because Meeker is a compulsive gambler, Spenser and Hawk travel to Las Vegas to look for him. They find Meeker with Bibi Anaheim, the battered wife of Marty Anaheim, who works for Fish. In Las Vegas, Shirley Meeker is found raped and murdered, and Ventura vows to kill his son-in-law. Spenser gives Bibi money and a plane ticket to Los Angeles to escape from her husband who has shown up in Vegas. Bibi disappears, and Russian thugs attempt to kill Spenser. Spenser and Hawk find Bibi back in Vegas attempting to retrieve money that Meeker stole from her. Spenser discovers that Anaheim stole from Fish and Ventura via Meeker, raped and killed Shirley, and put out the hit on Spenser. Hawk and Spenser trap Anaheim using Meeker and Bibi as bait. Spenser beats up Anaheim, has him arrested for Shirley's murder, and notifies Ventura of Meeker's whereabouts.

Small Vices (1997)

Rita Fiore, last seen as an assistant DA, is now working for a high-powered law firm, and she calls Spenser in on a special assignment. One of the firm's associates, Marcy Vance, once worked as a public defender, and one of her cases still haunts Vance. She represented a young black man named Ellis Alves, indicted for the murder of a college student, Melissa Henderson. Alves was convicted, but Marcy now believes that he was framed. Enter Spenser to investigate, and his brief is to find out whether Alves was really the killer.

No one really wants Alves back on the streets. He has a record of violent crime, including rape, but if he didn't kill Melissa Henderson, he shouldn't be in jail for that crime. Thus Spenser sets to work, assisted by Hawk. The more Spenser investigates, the more it becomes apparent that someone wants the investigation stopped. Spenser suspects the connection has something to do with the murder victim's tennis-star boyfriend, a young man who comes from a wealthy and powerful family. Figuring out who really killed Melissa Henderson almost costs Spenser his life, making this one of the most dangerous cases of his career.

While Spenser works on this case, he is also mulling over the news that Susan Silverman wants to have a child. Moreover, she wants Spenser to be the father. Spenser isn't certain that he really wants to take on the challenges proffered by rearing a child from infancy. Fearing that his relationship with Susan could be irrevocably damaged by his decision, Spenser has to weigh carefully how he will answer, and the plot of the novel underscores Spenser's concerns about having and rearing a child.

Sudden Mischief (1998)

Susan asks Spenser to investigate a sexual harassment case involving her ex-husband Brad Sterling, a charity fundraiser with a new surname.

The plaintiffs in the case rebuff Spenser, and Taft University law professor Francis Ronan, the husband of one plaintiff, sends thugs to beat him up. Spenser learns that Sterling's recent hyped event Galapalooza did not earn a penny for any nonprofit group. One charity, Civic Streets, appears shady, and Carla Quagliozzi, its president and another Sterling ex-wife, is killed and her tongue cut out. Sterling disappears along with a mysterious blue computer disk, and Spenser finds the body of a hit man in Sterling's office. Spenser discovers that the harassment lawsuit was retaliation by Ronan, whose wife was sleeping with Sterling, and that Richard Gavin, Quagliozzi's lawyer and lover, was laundering a loanshark's money through Galapalooza and Sterling. He finds Sterling hiding in Susan's house and deduces that Sterling killed Gavin's hit man and Quagliozzi because they knew about his skimming of Galapalooza's profits. The missing computer disk, concealed by Sterling in Susan's bedroom, contains details of the transactions. Sterling flees, but Spenser is confident that the police will eventually catch him.

Hush Money (1999)

Spenser is back on academic turf once again, when Hawk brings him a new case involving the son of an old friend. Robinson Nevins has been denied tenure in the English department at the university (unnamed, but presumed to be Harvard), and he wants to know why. Allegedly, he was denied tenure because of a homosexual affair with a student, Prentice Lamont, who committed suicide when the affair ended. Nevins denies the affair and denies that he is gay, and he has no idea why someone would circulate such rumors about him. Hawk has taken an interest in the case because Nevins is the son of trainer Bobby Nevins, with whom Hawk once trained.

At the same time, Susan Silverman asks Spenser to look into the case of a friend of hers, KC Roth, who claims she is being stalked. Recently divorced, KC doesn't know who is stalking her, whether it's a former lover or her ex-husband. She quickly begins to make a play for

Spenser, however, and he has to fend her off repeatedly while still trying to help her.

The further he delves into the Nevins case, the more complicated Spenser realizes it is. One of Nevins's fellow professors, Amir Abdullah, a convert to Islam and now a prominent figure in African-American studies at the university, piques Spenser's interest. Hawk knows Abdullah from some time back, before he changed his name, and Hawk has little use for him. It is Abdullah who seems to have started the rumors about Nevins's affair with Prentice Lamont, who was part of a group of three gay graduate students intent on "outing" persons who wouldn't officially come out. Eventually Spenser sorts out this very complicated mess, as well as the problem of the seemingly oversexed KC Roth and her stalker.

Hugger Mugger (2000)

Three Fillies Stables owner Walter Clive and his daughter Penny hire Spenser to discover who shot three of their horses. Clive fears that his young racehorse Hugger Mugger is at risk. Spenser travels to Lamarr, Georgia, where he has hostile encounters with Clive's drunk son-in-law Pud Potter and Three Fillies security chief Jon Delroy. Spenser discovers that Clive's daughter SueSue is an alcoholic, daughter Stonie was working for a madam, and son-in-law Cord Wyatt is sleeping with young male prostitutes. Walter Clive is killed in Three Fillies's exercise yard, and Penny fires Spenser. Clive's mistress Dolly Hartman hires him to uncover Clive's murderer and to discover if Clive's will includes a settlement for her son Jason. Spenser learns that DNA tests prove that Jason is Clive's son, and that Clive planned to draw up a new will that would give control of Three Fillies to Jason rather than Penny. Hugger Mugger wins the Hopeful at Saratoga. Spenser and ex-cop Tedy Sapp shoot it out with Delroy and his men. Spenser learns that Penny and Delroy staged the horse shootings, and that she told Delroy to kill her father, but Delroy will take the fall for her.

Potshot (2001)

Tourist service owner Mary Lou Buckman hires Spenser to find her husband's murderer in Potshot, Arizona. Mary Lou suspects that the Dell, a local gang shaking down the town and headed by the Preacher, is behind the murder. Spenser discovers that Mary Lou was sleeping with Mark Ratliff, a movie producer, and local police chief Dean Walker and seems to have ties to Southern California crime boss Morris Tannenbaum, who threatens Spenser. Bankrolled by town businessmen who want the Dell gone, Spenser gathers a posse composed of Bernard J. Fortunato, Bobby Horse, Chollo, Hawk, Vinnie Morris, and Tedy Sapp. Spenser learns that Mary Lou is a geologist who discovered a new source of water in Potshot and that the Dell was in Tannenbaum's pocket to drive people out of Potshot and lower real estate prices. He discovers that Mary Lou was sleeping with Tannenbaum and arranged to have her husband and Ratliff killed. Spenser and the posse have a successful shootout with the Dell when it pursues them. Spenser lets Dean Walker leave town with Mary Lou.

Widow's Walk (2002)

Spenser's friend Rita Fiore hires him to prove that dim-witted client Mary Smith did not shoot Nathan Smith, her wealthy husband. Armed-robbery suspect Jack DeRosa, represented by Ann Kiley of Kiley & Harbaugh, claims that Mary tried to hire him to kill Nathan. Felton Shawcross, CEO of a real estate development firm, threatens Spenser. Amy Peters, vice president for public affairs at a bank owned by Nathan, is fired for talking to Spenser and subsequently murdered. Spenser learns that Nathan was sleeping with boys, and his marriage was one of convenience. An attempt is made on Spenser's life. Brink Tyler, Nathan's broker, is killed after talking to Spenser, and DeRosa is shot to death. Spenser learns that Ann is having an affair with Conroy, who is involved in a real estate loan swindle. He shoots it out with the mastermind behind the murders.

Back Story (2003)

Paul Giacomin is back for a visit, and he has brought with him a friend and fellow actor, Daryl Silver, who is starring in the play Paul has been directing in Chicago. Daryl, whose real surname is Gordon, wants to hire Spenser to find out what really happened twenty-eight years before, when her mother was killed during a bank robbery in Boston. A revolutionary group, calling itself the Dread Scott Brigade, were responsible for the robbery and murder, and Daryl wants them found, since the police never seemed able to solve the case. Daryl can't afford to pay Spenser, but he agrees to take the case anyway, having recently been paid a large, overdue fee by Rita Fiore's law firm.

While he sets to work on Daryl's case, Spenser is mourning the recent death of Pearl the Wonder Dog. He drives to Toronto to pick up a new all-chocolate, fifteen-month-old female German shorthaired pointer. Her kennel name is Robin Hood's Purple Sandpiper, but Spenser and Susan name her Pearl. Pearl II quickly settles in with Susan and Spenser and becomes a member of the family.

Meanwhile, Spenser is having a surprising amount of trouble digging up some of the information he needs to progress further with Daryl's case. Daryl herself doesn't seem to want Spenser to delve too deeply into her own childhood, and the local FBI doesn't want Spenser to find out much about the case either. Never one to suffer such roadblocks lightly, Spenser naturally keeps digging until he gets results. The solution to Daryl's mother's murder proves to be very complicated indeed, and Daryl is left to live with the truth of a past she might rather not have known.

Bad Business (2004)

A beautiful woman, Marlene Rowley, walks into Spenser's office and asks him to find out whether her husband is cheating on her. Spenser takes the case, and it's not long before he has evidence that Marlene's husband, Trent, is indeed cheating on her. The strange thing, however, is that Spenser encounters another private detective who is working for Trent Rowley, trying to find out whether Marlene is cheating on her husband. From there, things continue to get more and more complicated.

There are, however, two common threads. The first is Kinergy, the energy trading company for which Trent Rowley serves as chief financial officer. The second is radio talk show host and advice guru Darrin O'Mara. Both Trent and Marlene Rowley and another couple, Bernard and Ellen Eisin, are disciples of O'Mara's, and their tangled relationships don't make Spenser's job any easier. Bernie Eisin is also an important executive at Kinergy, and when Trent Rowley is murdered, Spenser has to wonder whether the motive is personal or financial. Is everything at Kinergy as wonderful and profitable as it appears to be? Or is there something deadly going on? Spenser must trek through quite a labyrinth before finally hitting the center of the maze and discovering the complete truth.

Cold Service (2005)

As Spenser observes in the book's opening line, it started without him. Hawk was working as bodyguard for a bookie, Luther Gillespie, who was trying to hold out against the Ukrainian mob and their attempts to take over his book. Gillespie, his wife, and two of their three children are killed, and Hawk takes three shots in the back. Miraculously, none of the shots is lethal, but Hawk has months of recuperation and therapy to undergo before he can be his old self again. He also has tasks to undertake, because he failed in his job to protect Gillespie and his family. Hawk must seek out the Ukrainians who murdered the Gillespies and wounded him so badly and kill them. Spenser will be right there with him, just as Hawk has stood by Spenser for all the years of their relationship.

Finding a way to get back at the Ukrainian mob proves to be a complex task. They have the nearby town of Marshport completely under their control, despite the fact that the Ukrainians are only a tiny minority there. Tony Marcus, who runs all the black crime in the area, has an arrangement with the Ukrainians. Spenser and Hawk wonder why the very powerful Marcus would put up with such an arrangement. The answer to this question eventually gives Spenser and Hawk a way to accomplish their main goal, taking out the Ukrainians completely. The body count will be high before it's over, but once again Spenser and Hawk prevail.

THE JESSE STONE NOVELS

In 1997 Parker introduced a new series character, Jesse Stone. Stone has left the LAPD in disgrace over a drinking problem in the wake of his failed marriage, and in an attempt to get his life back together, he's taken a job as a small-town police chief in Paradise, MA. Struggling with alcoholism and his emotionally tangled relationship with his ex-wife, the actress Jennifer Stone, Stone tries to make a new life for himself in Paradise.

Night Passage (1997)

Jesse Stone leaves Los Angeles for Paradise, MA, where he'll assume his duties as the town's new chief of police. What Jesse doesn't know, however, is that the town is firmly under the control of several members of the Board of Selectmen, the town's governing body. Chief among them is Hasty Hathaway, bank president, and chief of a militia group, Freedom's Horsemen. Hathaway and his cohorts believe that Stone, because of his drinking problem, will be completely malleable. But when Stone begins to butt heads with the likes of Jo Jo Genest, a thug working for Hathaway, Hathaway and the Board discover that Stone is determined to do a good job. And if that means cleaning up the town, then he'll do it. He quickly finds allies among some of the members of the police department, like "Suitcase" Simpson and Molly Crane, while one member, Lou Burke, appears to have different loyalties. Following the murder of a young woman with connections to one prominent citizen, the violence escalates, and Stone and those loyal to him have to work fast to see justice done.

Trouble in Paradise (1998)

Stone has settled in well to his new job, and he has won the admiration of his department. He has been forging new relationships, dating some, but his demons still haunt him: his bouts of drinking and his unrequited love for his ex-wife, Jennifer. Trouble soon arrives in Paradise, in the form of an ex-con named Jimmy Macklin and his woman, Faye. Macklin has his sights set on a spectacular heist. He's going to take over an exclusive island community, Stiles Island, just off the coast of Paradise, and hold it hostage. He and his cohorts will pillage the homes of the island's residents, taking everything they can, then escape by boat. The plan seems foolproof, but Macklin has reckoned without Jesse Stone.

Death in Paradise (2001)

The corpse of a teenaged girl turns up, and Jesse Stone and his department try to identify her. When they eventually do identify her as Elinor "Billie" Bishop, they're stunned that the girl's family doesn't want to claim her. Stone perseveres, eventually getting information out of the dead girl's sisters. From there he digs deeply into the recent past to find every possible connection with Elinor Bishop. Early on Stone is called to the scene of a loud party given by celebrated novelist Norman Shaw and his latest wife. As Stone delves further into the case, he follows the trail to Boston and the offices of gay crime boss Gino Fish. The dead girl and other runaways had links to someone in Fish's office, and when Stone identifies the key figure in a nasty little prostitution ring, he finds the link to the murderer he needs.

Stone Cold (2003)

Jesse Stone has taken some important positive steps toward handling his two major problems, his alcoholism and his dysfunctional relationship with his ex-wife, Jennifer. Things on the job, however, remain complicated, especially when a series of seemingly random murders make life in Paradise more than a bit frightening. The odd thing about the case, other than the lack of any apparent links among the victims, is that there appear to be two people involved in the killings. A pair of thrill killers has come to Paradise, a husband-and-wife team who get off on filming their victim's last moments and replaying them. Stone follows evidence which leads him to Tony and Brianna Lincoln, an attractive, wealthy couple who have recently moved to Paradise. He strongly suspects that they are the killers, but will he be able to nail them before they claim their latest victim, Jesse Stone himself?

THE SUNNY RANDALL NOVELS

At the request of actress Helen Hunt, Parker created a character she could portray on the screen. Though a movie has yet to be made, the character of Sunny Randall has quickly become popular in the series of novels Parker has written. A private eye working in a Boston very familiar to fans of Spenser, Sunny Randall has appeared in four novels to date.

Family Honor (1999)

Gubernatorial hopeful Brock Patton hires cop-turned-PI Sunny Randall to locate his missing daughter Millicent. With the help of local crime figure Tony Marcus, Randall finds Millicent working as a prostitute. Millicent tells Randall that she overheard her mother order someone killed, and Cathal Kragan, the man to whom the order was given, saw her. Millicent moves in with Randall. Randall refuses to divulge Millicent's location to the Pattons and is fired. She learns that the Pattons cheated on each other and that their plumber, who had a liaison with Betty Patton, threatened to publish incriminating photographs and was murdered by Kragan. Thugs attempt to shoot Randall and snatch Millicent, and Randall's apartment is searched and trashed. She discovers that a major contributor to Patton's campaign is Rhode Island mob figure Albert Antonioni, and Kragan is his employee. Kragan attempts to kill Randall, who is protected by Marcus. Accompanied by her ex-father-in-law and local crime boss Desmond Burke, Randall meets with Antonioni and agrees not to blow the whistle on Antonioni and Patton. In exchange, Antonioni kills Kragan. Randall arranges for Patton to establish a trust for Betty and Millicent; Betty leaves her husband and moves toward reconciliation with her daughter.

Perish Twice (2000)

Sunny Randall's sister Elizabeth asks Randall to find out if her husband, Hal Reagan, is cheating on her. Randall tails Reagan to a woman's house and tells her sister that she should begin divorce proceedings. Elizabeth begins to follow Reagan, steals his car, and gets drunk at a restaurant where Reagan and his girlfriend are dining. Randall also learns that her friend Julie has been having an affair, is pregnant, and is going to have an abortion. Meanwhile, Mary Lou Goddard, CEO of a feminist organization, is being stalked and hires Randall as her bodyguard. Randall discovers that Lawrence B. Reeves, a former lover of Goddard's whom she denies knowing, is following her. Gretchen Crane, Goddard's research assistant, is murdered. Reeves is found dead with a note confessing to Crane's murder. Randall learns that Crane was investigating prostitution and that Goddard's significant other, Natalie, is a former prostitute and the ex-wife of local crime boss Tony Marcus. Natalie's brother Jermaine, who is employed by Marcus, attempts to kill Randall. Randall discovers that Natalie was sleeping with Crane and Goddard killed Crane for it. By Natalie's request Marcus had Reeves killed and shot Jermaine. Randall is unable to prove any of it.

Shrink Rap (2002)

Scepter Books hires Sunny Randall as a bodyguard for its touring romance author Melanie Joan Hall, who is being stalked by her ex-husband, psychiatrist John Melvin. At one appearance, Melvin smears his own blood on the front window of the store, causing Hall to faint. He follows Hall and Randall to California. Randall sleeps with Hall's west coast agent. She learns that Melvin treats only women, sedates them, and then he and his cohorts Dirk Beals and Barry Clay have intercourse with them. Beals threatens Randall, and there is an attempt to inject her with a hypodermic needle. Two of Melvin's patients die from drug overdoses administered by him. To catch him, Randall disguises herself and visits Melvin as a new patient, later consulting with psychiatrist Max Copeland about Melvin's treatment. Because Melvin has administered the paralyzing Xactil to previous female patients, Copeland prescribes Dilazaplin to counteract it in an effort to protect Randall, and Randall arranges backup with ex-husband Richie Burke. Melvin drugs Randall. He, Beals, and Clay attempt to rape Randall, but are foiled by Randall and Burke.

Melancholy Baby (2004)

Sunny Randall learns that her ex-husband is remarrying and begins therapy with Dr. Susan Silverman (from the Spenser novels). Sarah Markham hires Randall to find her biological parents, although Barbara and George Markham deny that she is adopted and will not undergo DNA testing. Randall learns that George previously worked at an Illinois radio station, along with now-famous TV talk show star Lolly Drake, and was known to have had multiple affairs. Thugs beat up Sarah, telling her to drop the matter, and confront Randall, who foils their assault attempt with her friend Spike's help. Randall learns that they were working for Ike Rosen, a disbarred New York lawyer, who was hired by Peter Franklin, Drake's attorney. George and

Franklin are found shot to death. Randall discovers that George relented on DNA testing and, when tested, found out that he was not Sarah's father. Barbara admits that she is not Sarah's mother. Randall learns that the Markhams received money every month from a shady corporation tied to Harvey Delk, Drake's manager. A letter mailed to Sarah before George died reveals that Drake is Sarah's mother. Randall learns that Drake arranged for George and Franklin to be killed to prevent disclosure about her illegitimate child.

THE STAND-ALONE NOVELS

Robert B. Parker's sixth novel, and the first not featuring Spenser, was *Wilderness* (1979). Since then Parker has written a number of nonseries novels, two of them featuring Raymond Chandler's famous private eye, Philip Marlowe. One is a love story, another is a western, others are crime novels. Thanks to his rigorous and productive writing schedule, Parker is now regularly producing two or three novels a year, and readers may happily expect more nonseries books in the future.

Wilderness (1979)

Aaron Newman, a successful novelist, is out jogging one morning when he witnesses a murder. Horrified by what he has seen, he assures the police that he will cooperate and help them nail the man responsible. The hitch is that the killer is a vicious man well known to the police, Adolph Karl. When two men enter Newman's home and tie up and threaten his wife, Janet, Newman tells the police that he was mistaken. Humiliated by what was done to his wife and haunted by his feelings of fear and inadequacy, Newman ponders solutions to the situation. Neither he nor his wife wants to live in fear of what Adolph Karl might do to them. With the help of Newman's friend, former Army Ranger Chris Hood, they plot to kill Karl themselves. After much surveillance and research, they decide they'll do it when Karl, his two sons, and a couple of his thugs head for the woods in Maine. There, in the "wilderness" of the title, Aaron and Janet Newman must face all their fears and the problems in their marriage if they are to succeed in freeing themselves from the threat hanging over them.

Love and Glory (1983)

Aspiring writer Boone Adams falls in love with mesmerizing fellow freshman Jennifer Grayle at a dance at Colby College. Grayle dates student Nick Taylor as Adams takes increasing refuge in the bottle. Grayle turns to him when she rejects Taylor's marriage proposal, and they confess that they love each other. Adams flunks out of college and is drafted and sent to Korea. He receives a "Dear John" letter from Grayle and begins to write unsent letters to her. Drunk, he attends her wedding to Cornell graduate John Merchent and is thrown out. Adams works in insurance advertising in New York and is eventually fired. He works his way west and, drunk and homeless, ends up in Los Angeles. He gets a job, quits drinking and smoking, works out, and writes in his journal. Learning that Grayle and her husband are teaching at Taft University in Boston, he enrolls as an English major at Taft via the GI Bill and remeets Grayle with the idea of winning her back. They become friends as they both work toward earning a doctoral degree. Grayle leaves her unsatisfactory marriage and her child for Adams.

Poodle Springs (with Raymond Chandler, 1989)

Private eye Philip Marlowe marries wealthy Linda Potter Loring (from Chandler's *The Long Goodbye*), and they move to chic Poodle Springs,

California, where Marlowe sets up an office. Local casino manager Manny Lipshultz hires Marlowe to track down photographer Les Valentine, who has skipped out on a gambling debt of a hundred thousand dollars. Valentine's wife Muffy claims he is shooting stills in Hollywood. In Los Angeles, the photos that Marlowe finds are nude photos taken by Larry Victor, a.k.a. Valentine. Marlowe learns that Victor has been blackmailing models with the photos and is a bigamist. Marlowe witnesses a fight between Victor and a blonde woman named Lola Faithful and later discovers Lola shot dead in Victor's office. Victor disappears. Clayton Blackstone, Muffy's father, tells Marlowe that Lola attempted to blackmail Muffy. Marlowe discovers Lipshultz dead, and the cops jail him for refusing to talk. Linda bails him out. Marlowe finds a compromising photo of Muffy taken by Victor with which Lola was blackmailing Muffy. He confronts Blackstone and Muffy, who pulls a gun, and learns that she killed Lola and Lipshultz. Muffy kills Blackstone, and Blackstone's thug shoots her. Deciding that their two lifestyles cannot mesh, Marlowe and Linda agree to divorce.

Perchance to Dream (1991)

Vincent Norris, butler to the late General Sternwood, hires Philip Marlowe to find Sternwood's troubled daughter Carmen, last seen in Raymond Chandler's *The Big Sleep*, who has vanished from Resthaven, a sanitarium. Carmen's older sister Vivian Regan and Claude Bonsentir, the head of Resthaven, deny that Carmen is gone. Marlowe learns that Vivian is dating gangster Eddie Mars, who previously tried to kill him. A vague Resthaven resident tells him that Carmen was involved with Randolph Simpson, a wealthy and disturbed oilman with powerful political friends; he learns that Simpson has ties to Bonsentir. A dismembered corpse is found that may be connected to Resthaven and Simpson. Vivian and Marlowe sleep together and are later beaten up by Simpson's thugs. Marlowe learns that Simpson is snatching up water rights in the desert at a pittance, planning to divert a river and make a hefty profit. Marlowe and Mars storm Simpson's yacht, where Marlowe learns that Simpson intends to kill Carmen. Amid a hail of bullets, Marlowe rescues Carmen and returns her to Vivian.

All Our Yesterdays (1994)

Parker's longest and perhaps most ambitious novel to date, this is the story of three generations of Sheridan men, Conn, Gus, and Chris. In 1920, Conn Sheridan is a member of the IRA in Ireland, with a reputation for fearlessness. He is badly injured during an assault on a police station, and while he is recovering, he falls deeply in love with one of his nurses, an American woman named Hadley Winslow. They begin a passionate affair, and Conn is so in love with her he is willing to forsake everything, even his commitment to the IRA, if Hadley will only come with him. Hadley, who is married to a prominent Bostonian, Thomas Winslow, refuses, and when the relentless Conn refuses to leave her alone, she betrays him to the police. His escape from prison is arranged, and he leaves for America, winding up in Boston.

There Conn Sheridan becomes a policeman, and in this role, he eventually encounters Hadley Winslow again. He now has the means to destroy her and her family, but instead he suppresses evidence of a violent crime, and he and Hadley resume their affair. Locked in a passionless marriage, Conn has long sought solace with other women. His marriage did produce a son, Gus, who follows his father into the police force. Conn dies in the line of duty, and he leaves to his son the evidence of the crime that could destroy the Winslows.

Gus Sheridan continues his father's blackmail of the Winslows, as well as the tradition of taking money from various criminals for "protection," and uses the money to build a better life for his wife and son. Like his father, Gus did not marry well, but he lives only for his son, Chris. Chris goes to Harvard, becomes a lawyer, and ends up teaching criminology at Harvard. He meets Grace Winslow, Hadley's granddaughter, and falls madly in love with her, unaware of his family's twisted relationship with the Winslows. When a turf war erupts between two Irish gangs in the South End, Gus, Chris, and the Winslows are all caught up in a situation which could lead to ruin for all of them. But Gus is as determined as ever to protect his son, and the chain of violence and obsession may finally be broken.

Gunman's Rhapsody (2001)

In 1879 young lawman Wyatt Earp takes his common-law wife, Mattie, with him when he follows his brothers from Dodge City to Tombstone, Arizona. There he encounters beautiful showgirl Josie Marcus, who's living with Johnny Behan, a prominent man in Tombstone. Wyatt no longer has any interest in Mattie, and he forsakes her for love of Josie Marcus, who returns his passion. Wyatt's affair with Josie causes problems with Johnny Behan, who uses underhanded methods to try to undermine the position of Wyatt and his brothers in retaliation. Wyatt, Virgil, and the other members of the Earp clan stick together amidst the shifting loyalties in Tombstone, a town riven by factions. This simmering feud ultimately leads to a deadly gun battle, now famous in western lore. In addition to the Earp clan, the novel features other famous "characters" such as Doc Holliday, Bat Masterson, and Katie Elder.

Double Play (2004)

After wounded Marine Joseph Burke returns from Guadalcanal, his wife leaves him for another man, and he turns to prizefighting and debt collection to pay the bills. Financier Julius Roach hires him to protect his daughter Lauren, who is being followed by her former lover Louis Boucicault, the unbalanced son of gangster Frank Boucicault. Burke kills two of Boucicault's thugs. Lauren and Burke sleep together, and Roach fires him. Branch Rickey, the Brooklyn Dodgers general manager, hires Burke to protect his new player Jackie Robinson, who is receiving death threats because he is black. Burke and Robinson confront gangster Johnny Paglia in a Harlem restaurant and Burke foils an attempt by Paglia's men to kill Robinson and his wife. Burke consults with black racketeer Wendell Jackson, who promises to deal with Paglia to protect Robinson. Burke then learns from Lauren that Louis Boucicault and Paglia have arranged for Boucicault to shoot Robinson in exchange for Paglia killing Burke. Burke teams up with Paglia henchman Cash to kill the gunman at the Dodgers-Pirates game at Ebbets Field and to remove Lauren from Boucicault's house. Paglia is shot dead by Cash. Burke tells Lauren that he loves her.

SPENSER ON SCREEN

A series of novels with such a fascinating hero is bound to attract the attention of Hollywood, and Spenser is no exception. Spenser first came to the small screen in the person of the late actor Robert Urich when the series *Spenser: For Hire* debuted on ABC. The first episode, a two-parter based on the novel *Promised Land*, aired on September 20, 1985. The series ran for three seasons, until May 1988. There were altogether sixty-six episodes of the show, followed by four television movies. The actor Avery Brooks made an indelible impression as Hawk, and there was even a brief attempt to spin the character off into his own series. *A Man Called Hawk* debuted on ABC on January 28, 1989, and ran for thirteen episodes, through May 1989, before being cancelled.

Spenser: For Hire featured some of the well-known recurring characters from the book. Barbara Block portrayed Susan Silverman in seasons one and three, Ron McLarty played Frank Belson, and veteran character actor Richard Jaeckel played Lt. Martin Quirk. In season two, Carolyn McCormick portrayed sexy Assistant DA Rita Fiore.

Robert Urich played Spenser in four TV movies, all based on novels in the series: *Ceremony* (1993), *Pale Kings and Princes* (1994), *The Judas Goat* (1994), and *A Savage Place* (1995). In the subsequent three TV movies, Joe Mantegna played Spenser, with Marcia Gay Harden portraying Susan Silverman. Two different actors played Hawk, and the character did not appear in one of the movies. The three movies, all based on novels, were: *Small Vices* (1999), *Thin Air* (2000), and *Walking Shadow* (2001).

A TV movie based on *Stone Cold*, the fourth Jesse Stone novel, aired in February 2005. Tom Selleck played Jesse Stone.

Robert B. Parker himself appeared in uncredited roles in two of the movies, *Walking Shadow* and *Thin Air*. In *Small Vices* he appeared as Ives.

For complete information on cast listings and other credits, those interested might consult the Internet Movie Database, a rich resource, at www.imdb.com. Information on the various episodes of the two TV series, *Spenser: For Hire* and *A Man Called Hawk* can be found on another terrific Internet source, at http://epguides.com.

CAST OF CHARACTERS

Each of Parker's novels contains many characters, and we have tried to include as many as possible of them in this index. The list is not comprehensive, however. Sometimes Parker does not name characters—for example, when thugs come to Spenser's office to threaten him, Spenser gives them descriptive nicknames. We have not included such characters, because there seemed little point in making an entry for a thug Spenser calls "Freckle Face." Otherwise we have tried to list as many characters as possible.

Aarons, Angie. (*Stone Cold*) Next-door neighbor of murder victim Kenneth Eisley, who tells Stone what she knows about her neighbor.

Abdullah, Amir. (*Hush Money*) Professor at the African-American Center at the university who appears to be behind the campaign to keep Robinson Nevins from achieving tenure in the English department.

Adams, Boone. (*Love and Glory*) Aspiring writer and protagonist, hopelessly in love with Jennifer Grayle.

Adams, Karl. (*Potshot*) Financial compliance manager at Southland Properties, trying to collect back rent from Jerome Jefferson.

Ahearn, Father. (*Thin Air*) Alcoholic priest from Proctor, who courageously helps Spenser despite what it might cost him.

Ainsworth, William, a.k.a. Willie. (*Hush Money*) Friend and roommate of Prentice Lamont and co-conspirator in the campaign to out prominent people.

Al. (*Hush Money*) A guy from Hingham who calls on behalf of his female companion to give Spenser information about her experience with being stalked.

Albanese, Sam. (*Double Deuce*) Head of the Boston Housing Authority; publicity hound.

Albrano, Charlie. (*Small Vices*) Evidence specialist for the Pemberton Police Department, who worked on the Melissa Henderson case.

Albright, Marcia. (*Sudden Mischief*) A volunteer for Galapalooza, she is one of the plaintiffs in the sexual harassment suit against Brad Sterling.

Alexander, Meade. (*The Widening Gyre*) Born-again Massachusetts Congressman running for the Senate.

Alexander, Ronni. (*The Widening Gyre*) The alcoholic wife of Congressman Meade Alexander, she is given to indiscreet rendezvous.

Alexander, Rose. (*Promised Land*) Radical feminist friend of Pam Shepard's.

Allie. (*A Catskill Eagle*) Bodyguard for the pimp Leo; shot by Hawk.

Allie. (*Double Play*) Bodyguard for mobster Johnny Paglia, knocked out by Joseph Burke.

Allison, Clay. (*Gunman's Rhapsody*) One of the gunmen who faced off with Wyatt Earp and lost.

Alves, Ellis. (*Small Vices*) A young black man with a history of violent crime, he is imprisoned for the murder of college student Melissa Henderson. Spenser is hired to figure out whether Alves was really the killer or the victim of a slick frame job.

Ames, Barry. (*Playmates*) Reporter for Taft University's newspaper, the *Taft Daily Collegian*, who breaks the story on point shaving by the basketball team.

Anaheim, Beatrice Costa, a.k.a. Bibi. (*Chance*) The battered, red-haired wife of Marty Anaheim, she runs away with Anthony Meeker to Las Vegas. Spenser is interested in getting her away from Anaheim.

Anaheim, Marty. (*Chance*) The unstable and mean associate of crime boss Gino Fish, Anaheim also beats his wife and is involved in a deal with Anthony Meeker.

Anathema, Pervis. (*Small Vices*) Pseudonym used by Spenser in an attempt to get information from the Pemberton College Alumni Association.

Anderson, Bob. (*Family Honor*) Framingham police detective who provides Sunny Randall with information on plumber Kevin Humphries.

Angelo. (*Ceremony*) Bouncer in the whorehouse presided over by Mrs. Ross; he proves no match for Spenser.

Angie. (*Wilderness*) Girlfriend of hired killer Steiger.

Angstrom, Arthur. (*Death in Paradise, Stone Cold*) One of the cops in the Paradise PD. In *Stone Cold* he gives Jesse Stone the glad news that members of the Board of Selectmen are there to see him about the serial killings.

Anthony. (*Pastime*) One of Gerry Broz's henchmen.

Antone. (*The Judas Goat*) One of the terrorists found dead in Amsterdam by Hawk and Spenser.

Antonelli, John. (*Thin Air*) Station manager at the radio station where Lisa St. Claire works in Proctor.

Antonioni, Albert. (*Family Honor*) Providence, RI, crime boss heavily financing Brock Patton's run for governor.

Antonioni, Allie. (*Family Honor*) Son of Providence, RI, crime boss Albert Antonioni.

Arlett. (*Playmates*) Insecure assistant DA for Middlesex County, called "an asshole" by Martin Quirk, who pushes to have Spenser arrested as a material witness in the murder of Taft University basketball player Danny Davis.

Arnold, Chuck. (*Small Vices*) Tennis coach at Taft University, where Clint Stapleton is his star player.

Atkins, Arthur. (*Potshot*) Principal of Fairfax High School, where Steve Buckman was football coach.

Augustino, a.k.a. Tino. (*Poodle Springs*) Half-Japanese, half-Hawaiian houseboy for Philip and Linda Marlowe.

Badyrka, Fadeyushka. (*Cold Service*) Member of the Ukrainian mob and one of the men with whom Hawk has a score to settle.

Baker, Arleigh. (*Trouble in Paradise*) Fire captain in Paradise, MA.

Baker, Glenda. (*Small Vices*) See **McMartin, Glenda Baker.**

Banks, Tommy. (*Valediction*) Owner/director of a dance company, with which Paul Giacomin has taken a summer job. Banks hires Spenser to rescue his girlfriend, Sherry Spellman, who has been abducted by a religious group, the Reorganized Church of the Redemption.

Bannister, Loren. (*Widow's Walk*) Nicely tanned CEO of an insurance company who tells Spenser the particulars of Nathan Smith's life insurance policy.

Barb. (*Love and Glory*) Fifteen-year-old sister of "The Shark." Boone Adams loses his virginity to her.

Barber, Red. (*Double Play*) Legendary baseball announcer, famous for using colorful metaphors.

Barnes, Luther. (*Potshot*) City attorney for Potshot, AZ.

Barry. (*Love and Glory*) Antiwar fellow graduate student of Boone Adams at Taft University.

Bartlett, Delilah, a.k.a. Dolly. (*God Save the Child*) Thirteen- or fourteen-year-old sister of Kevin Bartlett.

Bartlett, Kevin. (*God Save the Child*) Missing fifteen-year-old with a penchant for neatness and a resentment of his parents.

Bartlett, Margery. (*God Save the Child*) Flamboyant mother of Kevin Bartlett, with a reputation for sleeping around.

Bartlett, Roger. (*God Save the Child*) Father of Kevin Bartlett; owner of a construction business. He hires Spenser to find Kevin.

Bascomb. (*Double Play*) Black, white-haired lawyer involved in a proposal to pay Jackie Robinson to play in the Negro leagues.

Bataan, Eddie. (*Double Play*) Whistle-blowing Dodger fan.

Beale, Leonard. (*Paper Doll*) Broker from whom Spenser gets information on the financial status of Loudon Tripp.

Beals, Dirk. (*Shrink Rap*) Cohort of John Melvin in financial management.

Beaumont, Rich. (*Pastime*) Handsome new love interest of Patty Giacomin, who neglects to tell Patty just what kind of trouble he's running away from.

Becker, Abigail Olivetti. (*Chance*) High school friend of Bibi Anaheim.

Becker, Dalton. (*Hugger Mugger*) Big, slow, black sheriff's deputy of Columbia County, GA, involved in the investigation of shootings at Three Fillies Stables and Walter Clive's murder.

Behan, Johnny. (*Gunman's Rhapsody*) An important man in Tombstone and deputy sheriff of the county, he and Wyatt Earp become adversaries because of Josie Marcus.

Bellini, Mario. (*Bad Business*) Coworker of private detective Jerry Francis, who helps him tail Marlene Rowley.

Bellino. (*Death in Paradise*) Prisoner in the Paradise PD jail, arrested on a drunk and disorderly, who's making quite a ruckus until Jesse Stone persuades him to be quiet.

Belson, Frank, Sergeant (later Lieutenant). Sergeant in the homicide bureau who usually works with Martin Quirk. In *The Godwulf Manuscript*, he investigates the Powell murder. He appears briefly in *God Save the Child*. In *Mortal Stakes* he brings Spenser a tip that Frank Doerr wants Spenser dead. In *Looking for Rachel Wallace*, he investigates Wallace's kidnapping and permits Spenser to rough up a suspect. In *A Savage Place*, he vouches for Spenser with the LAPD. He appears briefly with Martin Quirk when Spenser needs backup while confronting a dangerous businessman in *Ceremony*. In *The Widening Gyre*, he gives Spenser information on Gerry Broz. In *A Catskill Eagle*, he moves Susan and Rachel Wallace to a safe hotel room at Spenser's request. He comes to Spenser to inform him that the New York cops want to talk to him in connection with the death of Ginger Buckey in *Taming a Sea-Horse*. In *Crimson Joy* he and Quirk work with Spenser and Hawk to capture the serial killer terrorizing Boston. In *Double Deuce*, he gives Spenser information on Devona Jefferson's murder and later arrests Tony Marcus. In *Playmates*, he looks up Madelaine Roth's license plate number for Spenser and is present for the meeting in Quirk's office about the murder of Taft University basketball player Danny Davis, likening Spenser to Father Flanagan of Boys Town. In *Thin Air* his second wife, Lisa St. Claire, has disappeared, and at first he is determined to find her himself. Eventually, however, it is Spenser who must step in and find the missing woman and extricate her from a perilous situation. In *Chance*, he talks to Spenser after Spenser kills two Russians attempting to shoot him. In *Widow's Walk*, he brings Spenser in to question small-time thug Jack DeRosa. He helps guard Susan when Spenser is threatened by a hit man in connection with the Melissa Henderson case in *Small Vices*. In *Hush Money* Spenser consults him on the alleged suicide of Prentice Lamont. In *Melancholy*

Baby, he is called to the scene of George Markham's murder. In *Trouble in Paradise* he fills Suitcase Simpson in on Jimmy Macklin.

Belson, Lisa St. Claire. See **St. Claire, Lisa.**

Bender, Lewis. (*Melancholy Baby*) White-haired high-powered criminal-law attorney for Lolly Drake.

Benedetto, Robert. (*Shrink Rap*) Boyfriend of Sally Millwood.

Bennati, Mario. (*Back Story*) Now retired, he was the lead detective on the team investigating the bank robbery and murder of Emily Gordon back in 1974.

Benny. (*Looking for Rachel Wallace*) Belmont cop, the older and fatter partner of Foley.

Betty. (*Hush Money*) Secretary of Louis Vincent.

Big Nose. (*The Judas Goat*) Nickname given by Spenser to one of the terrorists in Copenhagen.

Billy. (*Double Deuce*) Stolid black bodyguard for crime boss Tony Marcus, described by Spenser as "the size of Nairobi" (174).

Birmingham, Allison. (*Shrink Rap*) Vice president for publicity for Scepter Books, Melanie Joan Hall's publisher.

Bisbee, Thomas. (*Widow's Walk*) Real estate appraiser roughed up by Felton Shawcross's men.

Bishop, Carla. (*Death in Paradise*) Younger sister of murder victim Elinor Bishop.

Bishop, Elinor, a.k.a. Billie. (*Death in Paradise*) Troubled teenager, disowned by her family, who is the murder victim Jesse Stone struggles to identify.

Bishop, Emily. (*Death in Paradise*) Older sister of murder victim Elinor Bishop; she's now a student at Mount Holyoke College.

Bishop, Hank. (*Death in Paradise*) Father of murder victim Elinor Bishop.

Bishop, Sandy. (*Death in Paradise*) Cold, unfeeling mother of disowned murdered teenager Elinor Bishop.

Bixley, Tony. (*Double Play*) Owner of Café Madagascar in New York.

Black, Raymond. (*Shrink Rap*) Blond LA sheriff's deputy.

Blackstone, Clayton. (*Poodle Springs*) Wealthy, hatchet-faced father of Muffy Valentine; made his money through gambling operations.

Blair, Mickey. (*Hugger Mugger*) A young, female exercise rider at Three Fillies Stables.

Blondie. (*Perchance to Dream*) Pasty-faced thug for Eddie Mars.

Blossom. (*Perish Twice*) A florist in Cambridge, proprietor of the Blossom Shop.

Bob. (*A Catskill Eagle*) A portly, red-haired security guard at Jerry Costigan's estate.

Bob. (*Chance*) A helpful hotel coffee shop waiter in Las Vegas who is from Dorchester, a suburb of Boston. Spenser overtips him for speaking with a Boston accent.

"Bobby." (*Double Play*) Conarrator of the novel; possibly attempted to assassinate Jackie Robinson.

Boc, John. (*Double Deuce*) Chief of the Boston Housing Authority police force. He appreciates Hawk's and Spenser's presence at Double Deuce.

Bonsentir, Claude, Dr. (*Perchance to Dream*) Disturbing head of the sanitarium where Carmen Sternwood is residing.

Boucher. (*Looking for Rachel Wallace*) Head of security at First Mutual Insurance, Boucher is punched out by Spenser.

Boucicault, Frank. (*Double Play*, "Harlem Nocturne") A gangster seeking to keep his son out of trouble in *Double Play*. He also appears in the story "Harlem Nocturne" as the racketeer who is confronted by Robinson and the unnamed narrator in a Harlem restaurant.

Boucicault, Louis. (*Double Play*) Abusive son of Frank Boucicault; lover of Lauren Roach.

Boudreau, Felicia. (*Paper Doll*) Detective with the Alton County Sheriff's Department, she keeps a close eye on Spenser's activities in her territory. In *Hugger Mugger*, she tells Becker and Spenser about a horse shot in her area.

Boudreau, Trudy. (*All Our Yesterdays*) Young murder victim.

Boyd, Father. (*All Our Yesterdays*) Priest who visits with Peggy Sheridan.

Boylan, Mickey. (*Stardust*) Transportation captain on the set of Jill Joyce's television show, being filmed in Boston.

Bradley, Don. (*Family Honor*) Egotistical and drunk lawyer for Cone Oakes who has one date with Sunny Randall.

Brady, Casper A. (*Love and Glory*) Dean at Colby College who expels Boone Adams.

Braves, Boston. (*Double Play*) The 1947 Boston Braves team that played against the Brooklyn Dodgers was composed of Mort Cooper (pitcher), Dick Culler (shortstop), Bob Elliott (third base), Tommy Holmes (outfielder, pinch hitter), Johnny Hopp (centerfield), Walt Lanfranconi (pitcher), Danny Litwhiler (left field), Phil Masi (catcher), Mike McCormick (right field), Tommy Neill (outfielder, pinch hitter), Bama Rowell (left field), Connie Ryan (second base), Sibby Sisti (shortstop), Earl Torgeson (first base), Johnny Sain (pitcher), and Warren Spahn (pitcher).

Breakenridge, Bill. (*Gunman's Rhapsody*) One of the sheriff's deputies in the party arresting Doc Holliday for a murder.

Brewster, Peter. (*Savage Place*) Head of Oceania Industries, the parent company of Summit Studios. Roger Hammond's boss, later lover of TV reporter Candy Sloan.

Brill. (*Hugger Mugger*) Employee of Security South who fails to prevent Spenser's entry into the Clive house.

Brocius, Curley Bill. (*Gunman's Rhapsody*) Cowboy who kills city marshal Fred White and an enemy of the Earps.

Brodkey, Herb. (*Stardust*) Lawyer for Zenith Meridien, which is producing Jill Joyce's television show.

Brooks, Elaine. (*Early Autumn*) Girlfriend of Mel Giacomin; in tracking her down, Spenser finds the missing son he's been hired to find.

Brooks, Owen. (*Small Vices*) Suffolk County DA who is called in for a crucial scene in the resolution of the Melissa Henderson murder case.

Brown, Cony. (*Sudden Mischief*) Hired muscle who threatens Brad Sterling; he later turns up dead.

Brown, Henry. (*Potshot*) Head of the Foot Hills Bank and Trust in Potshot, AZ.

Brown, Howard. (*Trouble in Paradise*) One half of the gay couple whose house is torched by local teens.

Brown, Mrs. (*Double Deuce*) A Double Deuce resident, she tells Hawk that the Hobarts took her son's lunch money and are hassling him.

Brown, Polly. (*Hugger Mugger*) The gay madam in Lamarr, GA; she gives Spenser information on Pud Potter and Stonie Wyatt.

Browne, Robert. (*The Widening Gyre*) Massachusetts Congressman and senatorial candidate who's on the take from Joe Broz.

Broz, Gerald, a.k.a. Gerry. (*The Widening Gyre, Pastime*) Eldest son of Joe Broz, Gerry Broz is a senior in political science at Georgetown University with quite a few extracurricular activities. In *Pastime* he's looking for Rich Beaumont and, unluckily for him, has to cross paths with Spenser. He is singularly inept in trying to follow in his father's footsteps.

Broz, Joe. (*The Godwulf Manuscript, The Widening Gyre, Pastime, Chance*) Local crime boss. In *The Godwulf Manuscript*, he warns Spenser off the Godwulf manuscript case. In *The Widening Gyre*, Spenser tangles with him about the illegal activities of his son Gerry. In *Pastime* Joe hopes that his son Gerry will be able to follow in his footsteps, but in his heart, Joe knows the boy is vicious, stupid, and incapable. In *Chance*, an aging Broz tells Spenser that Marty Anaheim put out a hit on him.

Brunelli, Sal, a.k.a. Tattoos. (*Melancholy Baby*) Scruffy thug who beats up Sarah Markham and tells her to drop the investigation of her biological parents. Spike beats him up.

Bubba. (*A Savage Place*) Muscle for Roger Hammond of Summit Studios.

Buck, Charlie. (*Night Passage*) A detective with the Campbell County, WY, Sheriff's Department, he investigates the burned-out truck driven by Tom Carson.

Buckey, Ginger. (*Taming a Sea-Horse*) One of the whores run by the pimp Robert Rambeaux. Spenser gets valuable information from her, and when she is murdered, he is determined to seek vengeance for her.

Buckey, Vern. (*Taming a Sea-Horse*) Abusive father of murdered whore Ginger Buckey, known as the "toughest man in Lindell, Maine." Spenser tracks him down in his search for information, then teaches him a lesson, a payback for his treatment of his daughter.

Buckman, Mary Lou Allard. (*Potshot*) Owner of a tourist service business in Potshot, AZ, who hires Spenser to find her husband's murderer.

Buckman, Steve. (*Potshot*) Husband of Mary Lou Buckman; murder victim.

Bullet. (*Sudden Mischief*) A short and thickset thug who attempts to pound Spenser without success.

Burke, Carole Duke. (*Double Play*) Girlfriend, then wife and ex-wife, of veteran Joseph Burke.

Burke, Desmond. (*Family Honor, Perish Twice*) Boston crime boss and Richie's father. In *Family Honor*, he protects Sunny from Albert Antonioni. In *Perish Twice*, he warns Tony Marcus off harming Sunny.

Burke, Ernie. (*Family Honor*) Boston mob figure; brother of Desmond Burke.

Burke, Felix. (*Family Honor, Perish Twice, Melancholy Baby*) Former heavyweight boxer and Boston mob figure; younger brother of Desmond Burke. In *Family Honor* and *Perish Twice*, he accompanies Desmond to meetings with Albert Antonioni and Tony Marcus respectively. In *Melancholy Baby*, he brings the person who shot George Markham to meet Randall.

Burke, Joseph. (*Double Play*) World War II vet and former boxer who hires on to guard Jackie Robinson.

Burke, Kathryn. (*Melancholy Baby*) Blonde second wife of Richie Burke.

Burke, Lou. (*Night Passage*) A long-time cop in Paradise, MA, he is totally loyal to Hasty Hathaway. He discovers that his loyalty costs him the ultimate price.

Burke, Mary Alice. (*All Our Yesterdays*) Assistant to the mayor of Boston, Parnell Flaherty, and longtime mistress of Gus Sheridan. She works behind the scenes to do what she can for Gus and Chris Sheridan.

Burke, Richie. (*Family Honor, Perish Twice, Shrink Rap, Melancholy Baby*) Ex-husband of Sunny Randall who runs several saloons; son of local crime boss Desmond Burke. He provides backup to Sunny in

Family Honor, *Perish Twice*, and *Shrink Rap*. In *Melancholy Baby*, he gets remarried.

Burlington, Donna. (*Mortal Stakes*) Spenser tracks her down in his quest for information about the past of Linda Rabb.

Burlington, Mr. and Mrs. (*Mortal Stakes*) Elderly, colorless parents of Donna Burlington, who left her home and Redford, IL, behind years before.

Burns, Jim. (*Stone Cold*) One of the Board of Selectmen who visits Jesse Stone to express concern over the serial killings.

Burns, Maureen. (*All Our Yesterdays*) Young girl found raped and murdered; Conn Sheridan quickly finds evidence that gives him a hold over the Winslows.

Buster. (*Perish Twice*) Muscle for Desmond Burke with very little neck.

Butler, Ray. (*Potshot*) Water resource person for Chiricahuas County, AZ.

Caldwell, Katherine. (*The Judas Goat*) Name used by the female member of the terrorist group Liberty and the member Spenser uses as the "judas goat" to flush out the rest.

Callahan. (*Looking for Rachel Wallace*) Assistant night manager (a.k.a. "house dick") at the Ritz where Rachel Wallace is staying.

Callahan, Billy. (*All Our Yesterdays*) Gus Sheridan's driver and loyal associate; not very bright, but he'll do anything for Gus.

Callahan, Morris. (*Stardust*) Lawyer for the network on which actress Jill Joyce's show airs.

Cambell, Tom. (*The Widening Gyre*) Thick-necked cop assigned to security detail for Congressman Meade Alexander.

Cameron, Mrs. (*Small Vices*) Housemother at the Phi Gam sorority at Pemberton College, she takes a dim view of Spenser's attempt to question Melissa Henderson's sorority sisters.

Campbell, Marcy. (*Trouble in Paradise, Stone Cold*) Attractive real estate agent who is showing Macklin and Faye around on Stiles Island. She has a brief fling with Jesse Stone. In *Stone Cold* she and Jesse are still seeing each other.

Canton, Alex. (*Trouble in Paradise*) One half of a gay couple whose house is torched by local teens.

Captain Cat. (*Night Passage*) Feline that has taken up an all-too-brief residence in the Paradise PD.

Cardinals, St. Louis. (*Double Play*) The 1947 St. Louis Cardinals roster that played against the Brooklyn Dodgers was composed of Erv Dusak (left field), Whitey Kurowski (third base), Marty Marion (shortstop), Joe Medwick (right field), Terry Moore (centerfield), Stan Musial (first base), Ron Northey (right field), Howie Pollet (pitcher), Del Rice (catcher), Red Schoendienst (second base), and Enos Slaughter (left field).

Carey, Barbara. (*Stone Cold*) Second victim of the serial killers.

Carmichael, Foster. (*Ceremony*) An associate commissioner of education, he's caught in a very compromising position.

Carroll, Jason. (*The Judas Goat*) Hugh Dixon's attorney, who handles the money for Spenser's assignment.

Carson, Tom. (*Night Passage*) Former chief of police in Paradise, he finds that retirement can be a lot more dangerous than he planned.

Carter, Billy. (*Mortal Stakes*) Redheaded, smart-mouthed catcher for the Boston Red Sox.

Cartwright, Paige. (*The Widening Gyre*) Girlfriend of Paul Giacomin.

Cash. (*Double Play*) Thin, high-shouldered shooter for Johnny Paglia.

Cassidy, John. (*All Our Yesterdays*) Cop working with Gus Sheridan on the South End gang killings.

Cassidy, Shannon. (*Stardust*) Name of the psychiatrist that actress Jill Joyce portrays in her television series.

Cataldo, Lonnie. (*Ceremony*) Cop in Smithfield who helps Spenser search for information about April Kyle by taking him to find Hummer and the other "bad kids" he hangs out with.

Cecile. (*Bad Business*, *Cold Service*) Attractive black surgeon who's involved with Hawk; in *Bad Business* she agrees to help Spenser by doing some unusual undercover work. In *Cold Service* she has to decide whether she can continue her relationship with Hawk or break it off.

Cesar. (*Pale Kings and Princes*) Muscle for Wheaton businessman Felipe Esteva.

Chambers, Royette. (*Crimson Joy*) One of the victims of the Red Rose Killer.

Chang, Bo. (*Trouble in Paradise*) Sleek Asian man who's doing a drug deal with Crow, one of Macklin's gang.

Chantelle. (*Crimson Joy*) One of the victims of the Red Rose Killer.

Chapin, Malcolm. (*Paper Doll*) Chief aide to Senator Bob Stratton, he is mentioned numerous times, though he never actually appears in the book.

Chase, Miss. (*Valediction*) Receptionist at the office of the Reorganized Church of the Redemption.

Cheryl. (*Chance*) Flight attendant on Hawk's and Spenser's Boston-to-Dallas flight. She gives Hawk her telephone number.

Chester, Hilda. (*Double Play*) Cowbell-wielding baseball fan.

Chico. (*A Catskill Eagle*) Lean, black Transpan worker in Pequod, CT, who gets beaten in arm wrestling by his coworker Red.

Chollo. (*Stardust, Thin Air, Chance, Potshot*) One of the associates of Los Angeles crime boss Victor del Rio. In *Thin Air* he comes east to help Spenser, in Hawk's absence, when Spenser has to confront Luis Deleon in his stronghold. In *Chance*, he is supposed to pick up Bibi Anaheim in Los Angeles; she gives him the slip. In *Potshot*, he joins Spenser's posse to rid Potshot, AZ, of the gang called the Dell.

Christopher, Tommy. (*Playmates*) Acquaintance of Spenser's from the Harbor Health Club and a former DePaul and Celtics basketball player and coach at Providence College. He provides expert opinion on incidents of point shaving to Spenser by watching past games of the Taft University basketball team with Spenser.

Christopholous, Demetrius, a.k.a. Jimmy. (*Walking Shadow*) Artistic director of the Port City Theater Company and master schmoozer who is being stalked.

Chuck. (*Double Play*) Assassin who makes an attempt on Jackie Robinson; Joseph Burke shoots him.

Chuckie. (*Chance*) Bay Village pimp who gives Spenser information on a henchman of Tony Marcus.

Cimoli, Henry. Muscular, short owner of the Harbor Health Club, where both Spenser and Hawk work out. A former lightweight fighter, Henry often serves as a contact between Hawk and Spenser, especially in the early books. He appears briefly in almost every book in the series. In *God Save the Child*, he provides information on Vic Harroway to Spenser. In *A Catskill Eagle*, he provides a fake cast to Spenser as part of a plan to break Hawk out of jail. In *Chance*, he stores Hawk's gun for him while he is away in San Antonio. In *Sudden Mischief*, he provides transportation for the prostitute Velvet so Spenser can talk to her client Haskell Wechsler. In *Potshot*, he threatens to double Hawk and Spenser's (free) membership fee in the club. In *Widow's Walk*, he gets Hawk on the phone to talk to Spenser.

Clancy, Jerry, Deputy Superintendent. (*Crimson Joy*) One of Martin Quirk's superiors, he brings a group of concerned citizens to converse with Quirk and air their concerns about the investigation into the Red Rose killings.

Clanton, Billy. (*Gunman's Rhapsody*) Killed in the gunfight at the corral.

Clanton, Ike. (*Gunman's Rhapsody*) A blow-hard rancher, he has no love for the Earps.

Clark, Dennis. (*Back Story*) FBI agent in L.A. who goes along unofficially when Spenser and others call on Leon Holton.

Clarke. (*Sudden Mischief*) Former marshal employed as a bodyguard by Richard Gavin.

Clausen, Wendy. (*Perchance to Dream*) A pretty and friendly redhead, she owns the River Run Inn in Neville Valley and provides information to Marlowe on Neville Realty.

Clay, Barry. (*Shrink Rap*) Allergist cohort of John Melvin.

Clayman, Mattie. (*Sudden Mischief*) Director of an AIDS support organization, she tells Spenser that she did not receive any proceeds from Galapalooza.

Clive, Penny. (*Hugger Mugger*) Daughter of Walter Clive, she runs the day-to-day operations of Three Fillies Stables.

Clive, Walter. (*Hugger Mugger*) Owner of Three Fillies Stables in Georgia, which houses the horse Hugger Mugger. He hires Spenser to look into the mysterious shootings of horses at his barns and is later murdered.

Cockburn, Mildred, Dr. (*Paper Doll*) A psychotherapist, she was counseling Olivia Nelson.

Cody, Swisher. (*Looking for Rachel Wallace*) Cohort of Mingo Mulready; he tries to run Spenser off the road with Michael Mulready.

Colby, Jocelyn. (*Walking Shadow*) Tall, violet-eyed actress in the Port City Theater Company with a crush on Spenser and a claim of being stalked.

Coleman, Cecil. (*Perchance to Dream*) Chief of police in Rancho Springs, he leans on Spenser and Pauline Snow.

Collela, Dorothy. (*Looking for Rachel Wallace*) An employee at First Mutual Insurance who invites Rachel Wallace to speak to a caucus of female colleagues on their lunch hour.

Colley. (*Perish Twice*) Freckle-faced muscle for Desmond Burke.

Collins, Margie. (*Cold Service*) An Assistant DA in Suffolk County, who's working on a case involving the Ukrainian mob.

Collins, Michael. (*All Our Yesterdays*) The famous IRA leader who is later assassinated; Conn Sheridan has a brief meeting with him before fleeing to America.

Comden, Morris. (*Trouble in Paradise, Stone Cold*) Chairman of the Board of Selectmen of Paradise, MA. In *Stone Cold* he visits Jesse Stone, along with two other members of the board, to express concern over the serial killings.

Congo, Kid. (*Double Play*) A rangy black fighter, he knocks out Joseph Burke in the ring in the fifth round.

Connelly, Catherine, a.k.a. Cathy. (*The Godwulf Manuscript*) Former roommate of Terry Orchard; lover of Lowell Hayden; murder victim.

Conroy, Marvin. (*Widow's Walk*) CEO of Pequod Savings & Loan.

Coolidge, Gretchen. (*Taming a Sea-Horse*) With an MBA from the Wharton School, she seems proud of her job working with Perry Lehman, pornographer and proprietor of the Crown Prince Club.

Cooper. (*Chance*) Young detective with Las Vegas homicide who is assigned to Shirley Meeker's murder.

Cooper, Bob. (*Bad Business*) The CEO of Kinergy, he's got a lot of charm, but he doesn't seem to have a clue about what's really going on in his company.

Cooper, John. (*All Our Yesterdays*) Goverment official in Dublin assassinated by Conn Sheridan.

Cooper, Wilma. (*Bad Business*) Wife of Ben Cooper who seems very little concerned about what's going on at Kinergy; Spenser refers to her as "Big Wilma" after hearing Adele McCallister call her that.

Copeland, Maxwell. (*Shrink Rap*, *Melancholy Baby*) Psychiatrist recommended by Julie who provides insight to Sunny Randall on John Melvin in *Shrink Rap*. In *Melancholy Baby*, he tells Randall that he is retiring and refers her to Susan Silverman.

Corsetti, Eugene, Detective Second Grade. (*Taming a Sea-Horse*, *Small Vices*, *Playmates*, *Melancholy Baby*) New York City cop investigating the murder of Robert Rambeaux in *Taming a Sea Horse*. In *Small Vices* Spenser calls on him for help when he has a spot of bother with the hit man Rugar. In *Playmates*, Corsetti refers Spenser to Brooklyn detective Kevin Maguire when Spenser calls looking for details on wiseguy Bobby Deegan. In *Melancholy Baby*, Corsetti is working on the murder of Peter Franklin.

Cort, Adrian. (*Playmates*) President of Taft University.

Cosgrove, Wayne. (*The Widening Gyre*, *Valediction*, *Crimson Joy*, *Paper Doll*) Reporter for the *Boston Globe* with information for Spenser on Congressman Robert Browne in *The Widening Gyre*. In *Valediction* he once again serves as Spenser's contact at the *Globe*. In *Crimson Joy* he seeks information from Spenser about the Red Rose Killer. Now writing a political column in *Paper Doll*, he tells Spenser and Detective Lee Farrell all about Senator Bob Stratton.

Costa, Freddie. (*Trouble in Paradise*) Sailor recruited by Macklin for his scheme to hold Stiles Island hostage.

Costa, Steve. (*Crimson Joy*) Cop who checks Susan Silverman out when she qualifies for a gun license.

Costigan, Grace. (*A Catskill Eagle*) Fat, clinging mother of Russell Costigan; wife of Jerry Costigan.

Costigan, Jerry. (*A Catskill Eagle*) Arms dealer father of Russell Costigan; owner of a company called Transpan.

Costigan, Russell. (*A Catskill Eagle*) Susan's boyfriend; son of Jerry and Grace Costigan.

Costigan, Tyler Smithson. (*A Catskill Eagle*) Estranged wife of Russell Costigan. She provides information to Spenser on Russell and his family.

Cotter, Reverend. (*Night Passage*) He receives some rather embarrassing mail at the Episcopal church in Paradise and calls Jesse Stone to talk about it.

Cotton, Harry. (*Early Autumn*) Crooked used car dealer connected to Mel Giacomin. Spenser finds a good use for the information that Mel has such bad connections.

Coulter, Amy. (*Hush Money*) Social worker who talks to KC Roth after she's been sexually assaulted.

Court, Stephen. (*Early Autumn*) Boyfriend of Patty Giacomin; he'd just as soon have Patty's son Paul stay with his father.

Cox, Eddie. (*Death in Paradise*) One of the patrol cops in Paradise, MA, who helps search the site where the corpse is found.

Coyote. (*Back Story*) See **Holton, Leon James.**

Craig, Ken. (*Stardust*) Based in Los Angeles, he is actress Jill Joyce's agent.

Crane, Gretchen. (*Perish Twice*) Research assistant of Mary Lou Goddard; murder victim.

Crane, Molly. (*Night Passage, Trouble in Paradise, Death in Paradise, Stone Cold, Back Story*) Police officer and dispatcher who runs the front desk at the Paradise PD. She quickly becomes an ally of Jesse Stone's, and the two often flirt good-naturedly. In *Stone Cold* she plays an important part in the Candace Pennington rape case. In *Back Story* she calls Spenser to give him information Jesse Stone wants him to have.

Crawford, Dennis. (*Hush Money*) Birth name of Amir Abdullah, and the name under which Hawk first encountered him.

Crawford, Kerry. (*Shrink Rap*) Real estate agent and ex-husband of Kim Crawford.

Crawford, Kim. (*Shrink Rap*) Divorced patient of John Melvin's; murder victim.

Croft, Bobby. (*Wilderness*) State police detective who is handling the murder case reported by Aaron Newman.

Croft, Dr. Ray. (*God Save the Child*) The Bartletts' family doctor.

Cronin. (*Looking for Rachel Wallace*) Self-important Suffolk County assistant prosecutor, described by Spenser as "a twerp."

Cronjager, Captain. (*Night Passage*) Jesse Stone's boss at the LAPD.

Crosbie, Mr. (*Love and Glory*) Mean English professor at Colby College.

Crow, a.k.a. Wilson Cromartie. (*Trouble in Paradise*) One of the specialists Macklin recruits for his scheme for Stiles Island. He's a shooter.

Crump, Lieutenant Wilton, a.k.a. Buzzard Breath. (*Poodle Springs*) Sadistic, tobacco-chewing Riverside County, CA, chief investigator.

Cubs, Chicago. (*Double Play*) The 1947 Chicago Cubs team that played the Brooklyn Dodgers was composed of Phil Cavarretta (first base), Bob Chipman (pitcher), Dom Dallessandro (left field), Paul Erickson (pitcher), Lonny Frey (second base, pinch hitter), Don Johnson (second base), Mickey Livingston (catcher, pinch hitter), Peanuts Lowrey (third base, left field), Clyde McCullough (catcher, pinch hitter), Russ Meers (pitcher), Lennie Merullo (shortstop), Bill Nicholson (right field), Andy Pafko (centerfield), Marv Rickert (left field), Bob Scheffing (catcher), Hank Schenz (third base), and Hank Wyse (pitcher). Note that some players played more than one position.

Curly, a.k.a. Bo. (*Widow's Walk*) Muscle for Felton Shawcross, he attempts to beat up Spenser.

Curtin. (*Melancholy Baby*) Entertainment attorney at New York firm Harrop and Moriarty.

Curtis, Carol. (*Mortal Stakes*) Journalist Spenser brings in to break the story behind Linda Rabb's scandalous past.

Czernak, Sigmund, a.k.a. Ziggy. (*Back Story*) Associate of Sonny Karnofsky and husband of Bonnie "Bunny" Lombard Karnofsky; he isn't happy with Spenser's attempts to question Bonnie.

Danforth, Ray. (*Trouble in Paradise*) Head of the state police's SWAT team who comes to help out with the situation on Stiles Island.

Dark, Cawley. (*Potshot*) Leathery-looking chief homicide investigator for the Chiricahuas County, AZ, Sheriff's Department.

Daryl. (*Taming a Sea-Horse*) One of Tony Marcus's henchmen.

Davis, Danny. (*Playmates*) Guard on the Taft University basketball team, suspected of point shaving; murder victim.

Davis, Dawn. (*Death in Paradise*) One of the young girls working for Alan Garner.

DeAngelo, Anthony. (*Night Passage, Stone Cold*) One of the young patrol cops in the Paradise PD. In *Stone Cold* he is the one who finds Abby Taylor's body. Later, he is killed by Tony and Brianna Lincoln when he attempts to stop them from fleeing.

Deegan, Bobby. (*Playmates*) Brooklyn "wiseguy" profiting from point shaving at Taft University. He attempts to bribe Spenser to end his investigation and then tries to hire Hawk to kill Spenser.

Delaney. (*Thin Air*) Ineffectual chief of police in Proctor, MA, with whom Spenser consults in his search for information about Luis Deleon.

Delaney, Stuart. (*Playmates*) Young Walford, MA, cop involved in the investigation of the murder of Taft University basketball player Danny Davis. He arrests Spenser as a material witness.

Deleon, Luis. (*Thin Air*) Handsome former lover of Lisa St. Claire, he now fancies himself a crime boss in Marblehead, MA.

Delk, Harvey. (*Melancholy Baby*) Manager of TV talk show star Lolly Drake.

Del Rio, Amanda. (*Stardust*) Daughter of Victor del Rio and actress Jill Joyce, she has no idea who her real mother is.

Del Rio, Victor. (*Stardust*, *Potshot*, *Thin Air*) Head of the Hispanic rackets in Los Angeles, he has a special connection to actress Jill Joyce. In *Thin Air* Spenser seeks his aid in confronting Luis Deleon.

Delroy, Jon. (*Hugger Mugger*) An ex-cop who is head of Security South, which is providing security to Three Fillies Stables, and lover of Penny Clive.

Deluca, Jamie. (*Widow's Walk*) Bartender and former high school classmate of Mary Smith.

DeLuca, Richard. (*Stone Cold*) Lawyer retained by Mrs. Drake in the Candace Pennington rape case.

DeMarco, Kathy. (*Family Honor*) Detective in the Providence, RI, Police Intelligence Unit. She provides information to Sunny Randall on Albert Antonioni.

DeMilo, Buster. (*Sudden Mischief*) Bodyguard for loanshark Haskell Wechsler.

Denise. (*Hugger Mugger*) Proprietor of Bella's Business Services, which is a mail drop for Security South.

dePietro, Tony. (*Love and Glory*) A radio operator with Boone Adams in their Army regiment in Korea.

deRosier, Chantel. (*Playmates*) Classy black girlfriend of Taft University basketball player Dwayne Woodcock who is trying to teach him to read.

DeShayes, Joseph E. (*Pastime*) Pittsfield, MA, cop who wants to know how Spenser got shot and ended up in the hospital.

Desmond, Connie. (*Double Play*) Baseball announcer who worked with Red Barber.

DeSpain. (*Walking Shadow*) Big, blond police chief in Port City.

Devane. (*Valediction*) Cop from the state organized crime squad who assists on the case against Paultz Construction Company.

Devaney, Lance. (*Bad Business*) A very close associate of Darrin O'Mara, he has some highly unusual interests.

Diamond, Ed. (*Wilderness*) Senior police officer who is one of the pair of officers who respond to Aaron Newman's report of witnessing a murder.

Díaz, Angel. (*Hugger Mugger*) Jockey for Hugger Mugger in the Hopeful at Saratoga.

Digiacomo, Frank. ("Harlem Nocturne") Owner of the Harlem restaurant in which Jackie Robinson and the unnamed narrator have dinner.

DiBenardi, Eddie, a.k.a. Ed. (*The Widening Gyre*) Henchman of Vinnie Morris with a deviated septum; he tries to kill Spenser and is shot instead.

Dix. (*Death in Paradise, Stone Cold*) Therapist whom Jesse Stone has begun seeing. In *Stone Cold* Jesse continues to talk to him.

Dixon, Hugh. (*The Judas Goat, A Catskill Eagle*) A wealthy man who lost his wife and two daughters in a terrorist bombing in London; he hires Spenser to track down the group and bring them to justice, one way or another. In *A Catskill Eagle* he gives $10,000 to Spenser at Spenser's request.

Dobson, Harry. (*Stardust*) A contact at the Department of Motor Vehicles, from whom Spenser gets some helpful information.

Dodgers, Brooklyn. (*Double Play*). The teammates of Jackie Robinson are Rex Barney (pitcher), Hank Behrman (pitcher), Ralph Branca (pitcher), Bobby Bragan (catcher, pinch hitter), Hugh Casey (pitcher), Ed Chandler (pitcher), George Dockins (pitcher), Bruce Edwards (catcher), Carl Furillo (outfielder), Al Gionfriddo (right field), Hal Gregg (pitcher), Joe Hatten (pitcher), Gene Hermanski (left field), Spider Jorgensen (third base), Clyde King (pitcher), Cookie Lavagetto (third base), Vic Lombardi (pitcher), Don Lund (left field), Rube Melton (pitcher), Eddie Miksis (left field, second base, third base, pinch hitter), Marv Rackley (outfielder), Pee Wee Reese (shortstop), Pete Reiser (centerfield, left field), Stan Rojek (third base, shortstop), Howie Schultz (first base; later traded to the Philadelphia Phillies), Duke Snider (centerfield, pinch hitter), Eddie Stanky (second base), Ed Stevens (first base), Tommy Tatum (right field; later traded to the Cincinnati Reds), Harry Taylor (pitcher), Arky Vaughan (third base, pinch hitter), and Dixie Walker (right field). Note that players often played several positions.

Doerr, Frank. (*Mortal Stakes*) Funeral-home operator with shady connections who doesn't like the fact that Spenser is nosing around Marty Rabb, inquiring about game-fixing.

Dolly. (*Thin Air*) Bartender at the Club del Aguadillano, headquarters of crime boss Freddie Santiago.

Donaldson, T. P. (*Mortal Stakes*) Sheriff in Redford, IL, where Spenser travels seeking information about Linda Rabb's past.

Doreen. (*A Catskill Eagle*) Skinny waitress at the Pequod Inn. Hawk claims (in fun) to be in love with her.

Dotty. (*Bad Business*) Secretary to Adele McCallister at Kinergy.

Downes, Phil, Inspector. (*The Judas Goat*) London policeman who briefs Spenser on the terrorist group Liberty.

Doyle, Jim. (*Double Deuce*) Counsel for the Boston Housing Authority.

Drake, Lolly. (*Melancholy Baby*) Auburn-haired former attorney and TV talk show star.

Drake, Mrs. (*Stone Cold*) Troy Drake's mother.

Drake, Troy. (*Stone Cold*) One of the three teenagers identified by Molly Crane as a rapist in the Candace Pennington case.

Dryer, Margaret. (*Hush Money*) Dean of student affairs at a college in Fitchburg, MA, where Milo Quant is speaking.

Duda. (*Cold Service*) Law partner of Husak who is vacationing in Miami while his partner takes the heat from working for Boots Podolak.

Dugan, Chuckie. (*All Our Yesterdays*) Cousin of Patrick Malloy who learns a lesson when he tries to threaten Chris Sheridan.

Dunham, Dixie. (*Playmates, Small Vices*) Excitable basketball coach for Taft University. He denies allegations of point shaving by his players and forbids them to speak to Spenser. In *Small Vices* he points Spenser toward the tennis coach, Chuck Arnold.

Dutch. (*Hugger Mugger*) The Clives' Dalmatian who is fond of Spenser because Spenser feeds him clandestine hors d'oeuvres.

Dziubakevych, Bohdan. (*Cold Service*) Member of the Ukrainian mob, who could help put some of his confederates behind bars, if he doesn't change his mind.

Eagen, Marge. (*Double Deuce*) Opportunistic blonde host of the *Marge Eagen Show*.

Earhardt, Elsa. (*Shrink Rap*) Executive director of the Boston Psychoanalytic Society and Institute.

Earp, Alvira Sullivan, a.k.a. Allie. (*Gunman's Rhapsody*) Wife of Virgil Earp, who doesn't approve of Wyatt's treatment of Mattie.

Earp, James. (*Gunman's Rhapsody*) One of the older members of the clan, who tends bar at Vronan's bowling alley in Tombstone.

Earp, Mattie Blaylock. (*Gunman's Rhapsody*) Common-law wife of Wyatt Earp.

Earp, Morgan. (*Gunman's Rhapsody*) One of the clan.

Earp, Virgil. (*Gunman's Rhapsody*) Eldest brother of the Earp clan, and the one they all look up to as their leader.

Earp, Warren. (*Gunman's Rhapsody*) Yet another of the brothers.

Earp, Wyatt. (*Gunman's Rhapsody*) Legendary lawman and hero of the novel.

Eddie. (*Ceremony*) Guy with connections in Providence, RI, who helps Spenser find April Kyle.

Eisen, Bernard. (*Bad Business*) The COO of the energy trading company Kinergy, he suspects his wife Ellen is cheating on him and hires a private detective to catch her.

Eisen, Ellen. (*Bad Business*) Wife of Kinergy COO Bernard Eisen, she's cheating on her husband with his co-worker.

Eisley, Kenneth. (*Stone Cold*) The first victim of the serial killers.

Elder, Big-Nose Katie. (*Gunman's Rhapsody*) Lover of Doc Holliday.

Ellis. (*Double Play*) Associate of black racketeer Wendell Jackson.

English, Lawrence Turnball, Jr. (*Looking for Rachel Wallace*) Head of the right-wing Belmont Vigilance Committee; brother of Julie Wells. Dubbed "Square Jaw" by Spenser.

English, Mrs., a.k.a. Momma. (*Looking for Rachel Wallace*) Mother of Lawrence English and Julie Wells.

Epstein, Nathan. (*Back Story, Cold Service*) Agent in charge of the Boston FBI office; Spenser seeks information from him on the Dread Scott Brigade and the robbery-murder case. In *Cold Service* Spenser discusses the Ukrainian mob situation with him.

Erickson, Christine. (*Stone Cold*) Former wife of murder victim Kenneth Eisley.

Erskine, Harold. (*Mortal Stakes*) Executive with the Boston Red Sox organization who hires Spenser to discover whether pitcher Marty Rabb is fixing games.

Esteva, Esmeralda, a.k.a. Emmy. (*Pale Kings and Princes*) Wife of local Colombian businessman Felipe Esteva; she is rumored to have been sleeping with murder victim Eric Valdez.

Esteva, Felipe. (*Pale Kings and Princes*) Colombian owner of a produce business in Wheaton, MA, and fond of cashmere, Esteva seems to have clear ties to the cocaine traffic in the area.

Estrada, Rose. (*Mortal Stakes*) Manager of a building in New York City where Donna Burlington once lived; she provides Spenser with some interesting information.

Evans, Deborah. (*Small Vices*) President of Pemberton College, who is determined to protect the interests of the school and its students.

Fahey, Anne. (*Back Story*) Classmate of Bonnie Lombard at Taft University who tells Spenser what she knows about Bonnie Lombard and the other young people involved in radical politics back in the early 1970s at the university.

Fairchild, Morton. (*Poodle Springs*) Husband of Mousy Fairchild.

Fairchild, Mousy. (*Poodle Springs*) Flirtatious friend of Linda Marlowe.

Faithful, Lola. (*Poodle Springs*) Blonde former associate of Larry Victor's; murder victim.

Fallon, Phil. (*Pale Kings and Princes*) DEA agent who gives information to Spenser on the cocaine traffic in Wheaton, MA.

Fancy, Abner. (*Back Story*) Black prison inmate who worked with the radicals who formed the Dread Scott Brigade; he later became leader of the group and changed his name to Shaka.

Farantino, Frank. (*Small Vices*) Attorney representing Donald Stapleton.

Farrell, Francis, a.k.a. F.X. or Fix. (*The Widening Gyre*) Campaign manager for Congressman Meade Alexander.

Farrell, Lee. (*Paper Doll, Small Vices, Hush Money, Walking Shadow, Sudden Mischief, Hugger Mugger, Perish Twice, Shrink Rap*) The homicide detective assigned to the Olivia Tripp case in *Paper Doll*. His partner is dying of AIDS, and he's going through a difficult time, trying to balance home life and work. He helps guard Susan in *Small Vices* when Spenser is threatened by a hit man during his investigation into the murder of Melissa Henderson. Spenser consults him in *Hush Money* about the case involving Prentice Lamont and his publication which outs closeted homosexuals. He helps fix up Susan and Spenser's Concord house in *Walking Shadow*. He also tracks down Craig Sampson's fingerprints for Spenser in *Walking Shadow*. In *Sudden Mischief*, he is involved in the investigation of Cony Brown's murder. In *Hugger Mugger*, he takes care of Pearl while Spenser and Susan go to Saratoga. In *Perish Twice*, he is called in to investigate Gretchen Crane's murder. In *Shrink Rap*, he provides information to Sunny on the contents of the hypodermic needle that she was attacked with.

Farrell, Ray. (*Mortal Stakes*) Manager of the Boston Red Sox.

Fay. (*A Catskill Eagle*) A blonde prostitute, Fay is forced to host Spenser and Hawk in her San Francisco apartment after they break out of jail.

Faye. (*Trouble in Paradise*) Totally devoted to Jimmy Macklin, she'll do anything to help him.

Feeney, Kevin. (*Stone Cold*) One of the three teenagers identified by Molly Crane as a rapist in the Candace Pennington case.

Feeney, Mr. and Mrs. (Mira) (*Stone Cold*) Parents of rape suspect Kevin Feeney.

Feldman, Barry. (*Stone Cold*) A Boston lawyer who, with Rita Fiore, represents the suspects in the Candace Pennington rape case.

Felice. (*Pale Kings and Princes*) Muscle in a Celtics jacket for Felipe Esteva.

Felicia. (*Pastime*) Nurse at the hospital in Pittsfield where Spenser recuperates.

Felton, Gordon. (*Crimson Joy*) Security officer and a client of Susan's who could possibly be the Red Rose Killer.

Felton, Mimi. (*Crimson Joy*) Ex-wife of Gordon Felton, who has some helpful information for Spenser.

Felton, Rose Mary Black. (*Crimson Joy*) Mother of Gordon Felton; her nickname is Blackie.

Felton, Sam. (*A Savage Place*) A producer for Summit Studios, he is seen paying off a mob henchman and later shows up as a corpse.

Fenton. (*Perchance to Dream*) A Coast Guard lieutenant commander.

Ferguson, Frank. (*Hugger Mugger, Paper Doll*) Manager of Canterbury Farms in Alton, SC. He knew Olivia Nelson as a young woman, when she worked at the stables there. In *Hugger Mugger* he is the owner of Carolina Moon, a filly who is shot.

Figueredo, Dr. (*Shrink Rap*) Brazilian doctor at Mary Murphy Hospital in Haverhill, MA, who declares Sally Millwood dead.

Fiore, Rita. (*Pale Kings and Princes, Widow's Walk, Valediction, Small Vices, Sudden Mischief, Back Story, Bad Business, Cold Service, Stone*

Cold) A red-headed, well-proportioned assistant DA from Norfolk County who is, according to Spenser, "the best-looking law person in Boston (myself excepted)" (*Pale Kings and Princes* 9). Susan Silverman describes her as a "red-haired floozy" and "Miss Predatory" (*Widow's Walk* 29–30). In her first appearance in *Valediction* she's an assistant prosecutor from the Norfolk County DA's office who assists in the case against the Paultz Construction Company. In *Small Vices* she's now working as a senior litigator for Cone, Oakes & Baldwin. She calls Spenser in to investigate the case of a possible frame-up, in which a young black man was convicted of the murder of a college student. In *Sudden Mischief*, she provides information to Spenser on law professor Francis Ronan and lawyer Richard Gavin. In *Widow's Walk*, she hires Spenser to find out if her client Mary Smith murdered her husband. In *Back Story* she helps Spenser get some information he needs on the Emily Gordon case. Spenser consults her in *Bad Business* to get information on Trent Rowley, because her firm represents his company, Kinergy. In *Cold Service* Spenser and Hawk seek her help for a plan they have in mind to help the one surviving child of murdered bookie Luther Gillespie. In *Stone Cold* she appears in Paradise to represent the suspects in the Candace Pennington rape case. She and Jesse Stone have a brief fling.

Fish, Gino. (*Chance, Small Vices, Potshot, Night Passage, Death in Paradise*) An angular, gay Boston crime boss with precise diction. In *Small Vices* Vinnie Morris, the professional shooter, now works for him. Gino provides some important information on the hit man known as Rugar. In *Potshot*, he permits Vinnie Morris to join Spenser's posse. In *Night Passage* he works a deal with thug Jo Jo Genest that leaves Genest holding the bag. In *Death in Paradise* Jesse Stone goes to Fish's office looking for information on murder victim Elinor Bishop, and there he encounters Fish's handsome assistant, Alan Garner.

Fishbein, July. (*Melancholy Baby*) Head of the shady Bright Flower Charitable Foundation and wife of Harvey Delk.

Flaherty, Jack. (*Early Autumn*) Insurance man in Chicago who gives Spenser some useful information in his quest to nail Mel Giacomin.

Flaherty, Parnell. (*All Our Yesterdays*) Mayor of Boston with his eye on a Senate seat.

Flanders, Michael. (*The Judas Goat*) Man from Hugh Dixon's London office who fills Spenser in on some necessary details and makes sure Spenser has the necessary gun permit.

Floyd, Art. (*Taming a Sea-Horse*) Competitor of Tony Marcus in Boston prostitution; Spenser seeks him out in connection with April Kyle. Floyd is connected to a pornographer named Perry Lehman, who has some nasty underworld connections.

Floyd, Lester. (*Mortal Stakes*) Young, attractive man with a violent temper who apparently works as a bodyguard to Bucky Maynard, announcer for the Boston Red Sox.

Fly, Camillus. (*Gunman's Rhapsody*) Proprietor of a rooming house, also a photographer.

Foch, Nina. (*A Savage Place*) Spenser's nickname for the elegant receptionist at Oceania Industries.

Fogarty. (*Thin Air*) The pompous Dean of Students at Merrimack State College, where Lisa St. Claire has been taking some adult education courses.

Fogarty, Brendan. (*Trouble in Paradise*) Lawyer hired to represent the Hopkins boys on the arson charge.

Foley. (*Looking for Rachel Wallace*) Young Belmont Police cop who served in Vietnam and cooperates with Spenser. He clears off protesters when Wallace comes to speak at the Belmont Library, provides information to Spenser, and is at the scene when Wallace is rescued.

Fontaine, Velma. (*Ceremony*) Hooker working for the pimp Trumps; she gives Spenser some important information about April Kyle.

Forbes, Bradford W. (*The Godwulf Manuscript*) Self-important university president who hires Spenser to recover the stolen Godwulf manuscript.

Forbes, Roger. (*Looking for Rachel Wallace*) Attorney for Hamilton Black Publishing.

Fortunato, Bernard J., a.k.a. Bernie. (*Chance, Potshot*) Diminutive, panama-wearing Las Vegas private detective hired by Marty Anaheim to track down Anthony Meeker and his wife in *Chance*. In *Potshot*, he joins Spenser's posse to rid Potshot, AZ, of the gang called the Dell.

Fox, Sergeant (*Poodle Springs*) Riverside, CA, police detective investigating the Lipshultz case.

Fox, Pharaoh. (*Family Honor*) Tall black pimp who works for Tony Marcus; murder victim.

Frampton, Randy. (*Bad Business*) Attorney for Marlene Rowley, who is contemplating a divorce.

Fran. (*Trouble in Paradise*) Red-haired explosives expert recruited by Macklin.

Francis, Jerry. (*Bad Business*) Private detective working for Trent Rowley, who hires him to tail his wife Marlene.

Francis, Mr. (*Perish Twice*) Assistant manager of Locksley Hall Motel in Natick, MA.

Franco, Bobby. (*Perish Twice*) A round Boston vice cop who gives Sunny information on Gretchen Crane.

Francona, Roger. (*The Widening Gyre*) One of Joe Broz's men, nicknamed "Vandyke" by Spenser because of his beard; he tries to kill Spenser and is shot by Spenser instead.

Frank, Emily. (*Stone Cold*) Lawyer retained by Mr. Feeney in the Candace Pennington rape case.

Franklin, Mr. (*Love and Glory*) Classmate of Boone Adams and Jennifer Grayle at Colby College, described by Adams as "very ivy" (7).

Franklin, Peter Winslow. (*Melancholy Baby*) Handsome attorney at New York law firm Harrop & Moriarity who represents TV talk show star Lolly Drake; lover of Sunny Randall; murder victim. In *Melancholy Baby*, described by Randall as "built like a bowling ball and . . . probably no softer" (202).

Franklin, Steve. (*Walking Shadow*) Orthopedic surgeon who works with Spenser to treat actor Craig Sampson when he is shot at the Port City Theater.

Fraser, Dale. (*The Widening Gyre*) Balding cop assigned to security for Congressman Meade Alexander.

Frederics, John. (*A Savage Place*) News director at KNBS and Candy Sloan's boss; described by Spenser as "slicker than the path to hell" (*A Savage Place*, 120).

Fritz. (*The Judas Goat*) Nickname given by Spenser to one of the terrorists in Copenhagen.

Fusco. (*Night Passage*) Go-between who brings Jo Jo Genest some cash that a guy wants laundered.

Garcia, Eddie. (*Poodle Springs*) Thug for Clayton Blackstone.

Gardella, Fiora. (*All Our Yesterdays*) Chief prosecutor in the Suffolk County, MA, DA's office.

Gardenia, Charles, a.k.a. Chuck. (*Perchance to Dream*) Seersucker-clad employee of the Rancho Springs Development Corporation and Gardenia-Tartabull Insurance and Real Estate.

Garner, Alan. (*Death in Paradise*) Handsome assistant and lover of Gino Fish. Jesse Stone discovers that Garner is running a little business on the side, and one which Gino will not be happy about. He is probably also the unnamed assistant to Gino who appears in *Night Passage*.

Garfi. (*Love and Glory*) Brooklyn kid in basic training with Boone Adams.

Garfield, Patty Jean, a.k.a. PJ. (*Pastime*) Owner of the realty company, *Chez Vous*, for which the missing Patty Giacomin works.

Gary. (*A Catskill Eagle*) Gray-haired security guard of Jerry Costigan's with an Uzi.

Gault, Tony. (*Shrink Rap*) West Coast agent for Melanie Joan Hall; lover of Sunny Randall. In *Melancholy Baby*, Randall mentions to Susan Silverman that he has just visited her in Boston.

Gavin, Richard. (*Sudden Mischief*) Lawyer and lover of Carla Quagliozzi; lawyer for loanshark Haskell Wechsler.

Gavin, Steve. (*Bad Business*) Head of security at the energy trading company Kinergy; his loyalty to his boss exacts a high price.

Gelb, Rosalyn. (*Perish Twice*) Lawyer for Mary Lou Goddard.

Genest, Carole. (*Night Passage*) Battered ex-wife of thug Jo Jo Genest.

Genest, Jo Jo. (*Night Passage*) Thug who works for Hasty Hathaway. He keeps harassing his ex-wife, Carole, and he plays a nasty cat-and-mouse game with Jesse Stone.

Gennaro, Mr. and Mrs. Eddie. (*Night Passage*) Parents of Tammy Portugal. Mrs. Gennaro reluctantly lets Jesse Stone have her daughter's diary.

Gert. (*Stardust*) Behind the counter at Tunny's Grill in Waymark, she gives Spenser information on locating Wilfred Pomeroy.

Giacomin, Mel. (*Early Autumn*) Bitter ex-husband of Patty Giacomin and father of Paul, who has hired thugs to take his son away from his mother out of spite.

Giacomin, Patty. (*Early Autumn*, *Pastime*) Unhappy divorcee who seeks Spenser's aid in getting her son Paul back from his father, Mel, who has taken the boy to get back at her. In *Pastime* she runs off with a new boyfriend, not letting her son Paul know where she is. She's unaware that her new boyfriend has some unsavory, and very dangerous, connections.

Giacomin, Paul. (*Early Autumn*, *The Widening Gyre*, *Valediction*, *A Catskill Eagle*, *Pastime*, *Small Vices*, *Back Story*) Unfortunate teenaged son of divorced couple Patty and Mel Giacomin, who seems little more than a pawn in the power struggle between his parents. Spenser takes an interest in him in *Early Autumn*, and becomes a surrogate son to him. Paul is a dance student at Sarah Lawrence College and comes for Thanksgiving and Christmas in *The Widening Gyre*. In *Valediction* he has come back to Boston for the summer to take a job with a dance company, and he gets Spenser a new case to distract him from the fact that Susan has left him for a job in San Francisco. In *A Catskill Eagle*, he tells Spenser that Quirk needs to talk to him. In *Pastime*, now almost twenty-five, he asks Spenser for help in locating his mother, Patty, who seems to have disappeared. He meets Spenser for dinner in *Small Vices* while Spenser is in New York City, trying to track down the elusive hit man, Rugar. He brings his friend Daryl Silver (a.k.a. Gordon) to Spenser to help her solve the mystery of her mother's murder nearly thirty years before in *Back Story*.

Giants, New York. (*Double Play*) The 1947 New York Giants team that played the Brooklyn Dodgers was composed of Buddy Blattner (second base), Gary Gearhart (centerfield), Sid Gordon (left field), Dave Koslo (pitcher), Red Kress* (shortstop), Jack Lohrke (third base), Ernie Lombardi (catcher), Willard Marshall (right field), Johnny Mize (first base), and Ken Trinkle (pitcher).
*Note that Kress is listed on the team in *Double Play*, although the *Baseball Almanac* states that he ended his career with the Giants in 1946. The *Baseball Almanac* also lists Kress as a pitcher, not a shortstop. This is more likely to be Buddy Kerr.

Gillespie, Luther. (*Cold Service*) Dead before the book begins, he is the bookie who hired Hawk to protect him (in vain, as it turns out) from the Ukrainian mob trying to take over his "book."

Ginsberg, Nancy. (*Sudden Mischief*) Sister of Brad Sterling, married to a dentist and tired of lending money to Sterling.

Goddard, Florence. (*Shrink Rap*) Bridge-playing friend of Emma Randall.

Goddard, Mary Lou. (*Perish Twice*) Bisexual client of Randall's who is being stalked; CEO of feminist organization Great Strides.

Goddard, Natalie Lister Marcus. (*Perish Twice, Cold Service*) Significant other of Mary Lou Goddard; former wife of Tony Marcus; sister of Jermaine Lister; former prostitute. In *Cold Service* Spenser and Hawk seek information about Marcus's daughter from her.

Gold, Morris. (*Small Vices*) Attorney in New York City who serves as a contact for those wishing to hire the hit man Rugar.

Gold, Sybil. (*Back Story*) See **Pritchard, Sybil.**

Goldman, Paula. (*A Catskill Eagle*) Lawyer with the San Francisco firm of Stein, Faye and Corbett who acts as Hawk's attorney while he is in jail for murder and assault.

Gonazalez, Ramon. (*Thin Air*) Second in command to Luis Deleon.

Good, Jeffrey, Dr. (*Pastime*) Chief resident at the hospital in Pittsfield, where Spenser is recuperating from a gunshot wound.

Goodfellow, Doctor. (*Gunman's Rhapsody*) Doctor in Tombstone.

Goodyear. (*Double Deuce*) Fat member of the Hobart Street Raiders.

Gordon, Barry. (*Back Story*) Husband of murder victim Emily Gordon and father of Daryl Silver.

Gordon, Daryl. (*Back Story*) See **Silver, Daryl.**

Gordon, Emily. (*Back Story*) Murdered mother of Daryl Silver and the center of the investigation that Spenser undertakes on Daryl's behalf.

Gordon, Sergeant. (*Stone Cold*) A sergeant of detectives in Toronto who allows Jesse Stone to see Tony and Brianna Lincoln while they're being held in jail.

Gordy. (*Poodle Springs*) Fat L.A. plainclothes cop who wants to haul Marlowe in for questioning.

Gottlieb, Marsha. (*Death in Paradise*) Name of the young woman who registered for a room at the Boundary Suites motel with Norman Shaw.

Gottlieb, Murray. (*Shrink Rap*) Hollywood producer interested in filming some of Melanie Joan Hall's books.

Goulet, Robert. (*Chance*) An actor/baritone singer best known for his role as Lancelot in *Camelot,* Goulet is spotted at a Las Vegas airport by Susan in *Chance.*

Graff, Larson. (*Widow's Walk*) Public relations consultant for Mary Smith.

Graffino, Ethel. (*Widow's Walk*) Guidance counselor at Franklin High School, Mary Smith's old school.

Gray Man. (*Small Vices*) Professional killer hired to stop Spenser's investigation into the murder of coed Melissa Henderson. See also **Rugar** and **McKean, Kodi.**

Green, Kenny. (*Playmates*) Off guard for the Taft University basketball team.

Gregory, Captain. (*Perchance to Dream*) Head of the L.A. Missing Persons Bureau, he is consulted by Marlowe regarding Carmen Sternwood.

Grieff, Patti. (*Pale Kings and Princes*) A stunning blonde friend of Susan's, she has dinner with Susan and Spenser.

Grimes, Edgar. (*Paper Doll*) An employee of a Washington, D.C.–based security firm, he's one of the men who tries to convince Spenser to back off the case in Alton, SC.

Grove, Abner. (*Widow's Walk*) An expert in finance law who provides information to Spenser on a loan-to-value scam.

Gurwitz, Amy. (*Ceremony*) Friend of April Kyle who has also fled suburban Smithfield, MA; now she's living in Back Bay Boston with Mitch Poitras.

Gus. (*Double Play*) Father of the narrator "Bobby."

Guze. (*Love and Glory*) Colby College fullback and classmate of Boone Adams. Adams writes a short story for him.

Hack, J. Taylor. (*Playmates*) Portly and well-tailored Francis Calvert Dolbear Professor of American Civilization at Taft University. He tells Spenser that he can't recall having Dwayne Woodcock in his class, although Woodcock received a B-.

Hall, Sergeant Eugene. (*A Savage Place*) Cop called to Oceania Industries after Spenser takes Peter Brewster hostage.

Hall, Melanie Joan. (*Shrink Rap*) Best-selling romance author who is being stalked by her ex-husband John Melvin.

Hall, Typhanie. (*Thin Air*) Best friend of Lisa St. Claire.

Haller, Vincent. (*The Godwulf Manuscript*, *Valediction*, *Playmates*) Nattily dressed attorney for Terry Orchard who is engaged by Spenser in *The Godwulf Manuscript*. In *Valediction* he assists Spenser in setting up a trust to help Sherry Spellman run a new incarnation of the Reorganized Church of the Redemption. In *Playmates*, Haller introduces Spenser to the chairman of the Board of Trustees for Taft University.

Hammond, Roger. (*A Savage Place*) Head of Summit Studios, reputedly in hock to the mob.

Hannigan, Tommy. (*Family Honor*) Cop friend of Sunny Randall.

Hans. (*Judas Goat*) Nickname given by Spenser to one of the terrorists in Copenhagen.

Hanson, Carter. (*Stone Cold*) One of the members of the Board of Selectmen who visits Jesse Stone to express concern over the serial killings.

Hanson, Olivia. (*Sudden Mischief*) Volunteer for Galapalooza and one of the plaintiffs in the sexual harassment suit against Brad Sterling. She takes a shine to Spenser, who takes her to lunch.

Harmon, David, a.k.a. Tommy. (*Hush Money*) Professor in the English department who is on the side of Robinson Nevins.

Harold. (*Early Autumn*) One of the thugs hired by Mel Giacomin to take Giacomin's son Paul away from his ex-wife.

Harris, Ms. (*Mortal Stakes*) Social worker with the New York Department of Social Services who provides information to Spenser in his quest to track down Donna Burlington.

Harris, Wilbur. (*Potshot*) FBI agent who gives Spenser transcripts of surveillance tapes of Morris Tannenbaum.

Harroway, Vic. (*God Save the Child*) Homosexual former bodybuilder who is leader of a Smithfield, MA, commune.

Harter, JD. (*Trouble in Paradise*) A "cracker" recruited by Macklin to provide electrical expertise.

Hartman, Buddy. (*Early Autumn*) One of the thugs hired by Mel Giacomin to take Giacomin's son Paul away from his ex-wife.

Hartman, Dolly. (*Hugger Mugger*) Walter Clive's lover; mother of Jason Hartman.

Harvey. (*Back Story*) Hired gun working for Sonny Karnofsky, who tries to persuade Spenser to stop nosing into the Emily Gordon case.

Hatch, Miranda. (*Hugger Mugger*) Sixteen-month-old child of Valerie Hatch.

Hatch, Valerie. (*Hugger Mugger*) An attorney, she hires Spenser to get rid of the man stalking her nanny.

Hatfield, Curtis. (*Widow's Walk*) Head of security for Felton Shawcross. Hawk decks him.

Hathaway, Cissy. (*Night Passage*) Promiscuous wife of Hasty Hathaway.

Hathaway, Hastings, a.k.a. Hasty. (*Night Passage*) President of Paradise Trust and chair of the Board of Selectmen of Paradise, he also is commander of a local militia group, Freedom's Horsemen.

Havoc, Cord. (*Poodle Springs*) Movie star and lush.

Hawk. Introduced in *Promised Land* as an ex-fighter acquaintance of Spenser's and an enforcer for loanshark King Powers, Hawk has a smart mouth equal to Spenser's, especially when he performs imitation plantation dialect. Spenser summons him to London to act as backup while he tracks down the members of the terrorist group Liberty in *The Judas Goat*; Hawk stays with him through the rest of the case, on to Copenhagen, Amsterdam, and finally to Montreal. In *The Widening Gyre*, Hawk protects Spenser after Spenser is shot and accompanies him to a meeting with mobster Joe Broz to watch his back. In *A Catskill Eagle*, Spenser breaks him out of jail, and Hawk helps him track down Jerry and Russell Costigan. In *Pale Kings and Princes*, Hawk accompanies Spenser to confront Felipe Esteva. In *Playmates*, he protects basketball player Dwayne Woodcock. In *Double Deuce*, he asks Spenser to help him remove a gang from the Double Deuce housing project and discover the murderer of a teenager and her baby. In *Walking Shadow*, he follows Demetrius Christopholous to discover who is following him, provides a back-up gun for Spenser in Port City, and shows interest in translator Mei Ling. In *Chance*, he provides backup for Spenser in the pursuit of Anthony Meeker. In *Sudden Mischief*, he watches the charity Civil Streets and Francis Ronan's house, ensures that no one is watching Brad Sterling or Spenser, and is dating a cardiologist. In *Potshot*, he joins Spenser's posse to rid Potshot, AZ, of the gang called the Dell. In *Widow's Walk*, he follows the Volvo tailing Spenser, shadows Marvin Conroy, and provides backup to Spenser when they visit Felton Shawcross. In *Cold Service* it is Hawk who needs Spenser's help as backup. Badly injured and having failed to protect a client, he wants Spenser to aid him in taking out the Ukrainian mobsters who shot him and killed his client.

Hayden, Judy. (*The Godwulf Manuscript*) Somewhat masculine-looking, protective wife of Lowell Hayden.

Hayden, Lowell. (*The Godwulf Manuscript*) Medieval literature professor in the university English department; lover of Catherine Connelly.

Healy, Lieutenant. (*God Save the Child*, *Mortal Stakes*, *Walking Shadow*, *Small Vices*, *Bad Business*, *Cold Service*, *Night Passage*) Investigator attached to the Essex County District Attorney's office, working temporarily out of the state police headquarters office. In *God Save the Child*, he is in charge of the Bartlett kidnapping case. He reappears in *Mortal Stakes*. In *Walking Shadow*, Spenser treats Healy to a steak so he can get background information on Port City police chief DeSpain. In *Small Vices* he is now Commander of the Criminal Investigation Division for the state police. He provides Spenser with information about the state police detective, Tommy Miller, who investigated the Melissa Henderson murder case. In *Bad Business* he's investigating the murder of Trent Rowley, the chief financial officer at Kinergy. Spenser and Hawk discuss the situation in Marshport with Healy in *Cold Service*, trying to come up with a plan to oust the Ukrainians. In *Night Passage* and the other Jesse Stone novels, he often drops in on Stone in the Paradise PD to cast a friendly eye over what's going on, since he lives nearby.

Hedrick, Mary Ann. (*Playmates*) Assistant professor in English at Taft University who gave Dwayne Woodcock a C+ in her class yet was unaware of his illiteracy.

Henderson, Melissa. (*Small Vices*) The murder victim in the case Spenser is hired to investigate to determine whether the right killer is in jail for the crime.

Henderson, Mr. and Mrs. Walton. (*Small Vices*) Bereaved parents of the murdered college student Melissa Henderson.

Henry, Captain. (*Pale Kings and Princes*) Potbellied captain of the Wheaton, MA, police force who threatens Spenser.

Herb. (*Family Honor*) Maitre'd at Spike's restaurant Beans & Rice.

Herman, Dave. (*Love and Glory*) Classmate of Boone Adams at Colby College.

Hernandez, Tom. (*Love and Glory*) Owner of a Los Angeles coffee shop where Boone Adams gets a job as a dishwasher.

Hickock, James Butler. (*Small Vices*) Alias under which Spenser is registered in the hospital after he is shot by the Gray Man.

Hilliard, Dr. Dorothy. (*A Catskill Eagle*) Susan Silverman's San Francisco psychiatrist who tells Spenser why Susan is in therapy and the location of Jerry Costigan's lodge in Washington.

Hogg, Wally, a.k.a. Walter Hogarth. (*Mortal Stakes*) Hired muscle and loan shark working for Frank Doerr, who threatens Spenser in his office.

Holliday, John Henry, a.k.a. Doc. (*Gunman's Rhapsody*) Gunslinger and friend of the Earps.

Holly, Buddy. (*A Catskill Eagle*) Spenser's nickname for a CIA agent who wears horn-rimmed glasses.

Holmes, Betty. (*Back Story*) Registrar at Taft University from whom Spenser seeks information in the Emily Gordon case.

Holton. (*Stone Cold*) State police technician who gives Jesse Stone some ballistics information.

Holton, Leon James, a.k.a. Coyote. (*Back Story*) A former lover of murder victim Emily Gordon, he now seems to be living the good life in L.A.

Hood, Chris. (*Wilderness*) Tough former Army Ranger who plans to help Aaron and Janet Newman kill Adolph Karl.

Hooker. (*Gunman's Rhapsody*) Rancher who provides shelter for the Earps when a posse is after them.

Hopewell, Carlotta. (*Potshot*) Boozy girlfriend of Jerome Jefferson.

Hopkins, Charles. (*Trouble in Paradise*) Father of miscreants Earl and Robbie Hopkins.

Hopkins, Earl. (*Trouble in Paradise*) One of the teens suspected of committing arson against a local gay couple.

Hopkins, Kay. (*Trouble in Paradise*) Mother of the Hopkins boys who refuses to believe that her sons would do such a thing.

Hopkins, Robbie. (*Trouble in Paradise*) Younger brother of Earl, and one of the teens suspected of arson.

Horse, Bobby. (*Stardust*, *Potshot*) Native American muscle who works for Victor del Rio; referred to as "the Indian" by Spenser. In *Potshot*, he joins Spenser's posse to rid Potshot, AZ, of the gang called the Dell.

Hummel, Carl, a.k.a. Hummer. (*Ceremony*) One of the "bad kids" in Smithfield, MA, he may be able to help Spenser track down April Kyle.

Hummer. See **Hummel, Carl.**

Humphries, Kevin. (*Family Honor*) Framingham plumber and lover of Betty Patton who attempts to blackmail her; murder victim.

Hunter, Sara. (*Potshot*) Former colleague of Steve Buckman's at Fairfax High School.

Hurley, Elayna. (*Small Vices*) Single mother and friend of Susan's who brings her daughter Erika to visit Susan and Spenser. This small taste of parenthood convinces Spenser even further that he doesn't really want to have a child.

Hurley, Erika. (*Small Vices*) Bratty child of Elayna Hurley.

Hurst, Lieutenant (*Gunman's Rhapsody*) Army officer on the trail of stolen Army mules.

Husak. (*Cold Service*) One of the lawyers hired by Boots Podolak to represent his men, particularly Bohdan Dziubakevych; his partner is Duda, who is prudently vacationing in Miami.

Ichabod. (*Potshot*) Bony goon who works for the Preacher.

Isaacs, Peter, a.k.a. Pike. (*Widow's Walk*) High school friend of Mary Smith.

Isaacson, Morris. (*Perchance to Dream*) L.A. attorney knowledgeable about water rights.

Iselin, Philip. (*Crimson Joy*) One of Susan's clients, who might be the Red Rose Killer.

Ito, Steven. (*Thin Air*) Psychiatrist at a state hospital in Pomona, CA, who fills Spenser in on some of the missing background of Angela Richard.

Ives, Elliot. (*A Catskill Eagle, Small Vices, Potshot, Back Story, Cold Service*) CIA agent, described by Spenser as resembling "a salt cod," who calls Spenser "Lochinvar," arranges a safe house in Charlestown, MA, for Spenser and Hawk, and bargains with them to kill Jerry Costigan in

A Catskill Eagle. In *Small Vices* he helps Spenser uncover the identity of the hit man Spenser calls Gray Man. In *Potshot,* Ives arranges for Spenser to talk with an FBI agent who has Morris Tannenbaum under surveillance. In *Back Story* Spenser once again seeks his aid in finding out more about the organization calling itself the Dread Scott Brigade. Spenser goes to him in *Cold Service,* seeking a tough guy who can speak Ukrainian, and Ives recommends an old nemesis, the Gray Man.

Jackie. (*Chance*) Driver and caretaker for Shirley Meeker.

Jackson. (*Small Vices*) Boat cop whom Spenser consults when getting background information on convicted murderer Ellis Alves.

Jackson, Charles. (*Taming a Sea-Horse*) Called "Brutus" by his boss, Perry Lehman, he works as a bodyguard/hired muscle. He provides Spenser some important information on Ginger Buckey and the set-up at the Crown Prince Club.

Jackson, Wendell. (*Double Play*) Black racketeer in Harlem. Burke asks him for assistance in dealing with Johnny Paglia.

Jaime. (*Cold Service*) One of the men working for would-be crime boss Brock Rimbaud.

Jane. (*Promised Land*) A violent associate of Rose Alexander's, described by Spenser as an Amazon. Spenser decks her when she attempts to use karate on him.

Jane. (*Love and Glory*) Hostess of a graduate student party at Taft University that Boone Adams and Jennifer Merchent attend.

Jasmine. (*Stardust*) Assistant to Ken Craig, actress Jill Joyce's agent in Los Angeles.

J. D. (*Pale Kings and Princes*) Tall, square, mustached sergeant from the Wheaton police force who threatens Spenser.

J. D. (*Poodle Springs*) California beach boy thug for Clayton Blackstone.

Jeff. (*Melancholy Baby*) Manager of Moline, IL, talk radio station WMOL.

Jefferson. (*Paper Doll*) Elderly servant to Jack Nelson who is well familiar with the skeletons in the Nelson family closet.

Jefferson, Crystal. (*Double Deuce*) Three-month-old daughter of Devona Jefferson; murder victim.

Jefferson, Devona. (*Double Deuce*) Fourteen-year-old mother of Crystal and girlfriend of Tallboy; murder victim.

Jefferson, Emmy. (*Perish Twice*) Black cop who attended the police academy with Sunny Randall.

Jefferson, Jerome. (*Potshot*) Surfer-looking thug of Morris Tannenbaum who attempts to rough up Spenser in Santa Monica.

Jeffries, Herb. (*Double Play*) Singer at the Plantation in Harlem.

Jencks, Carleton, Jr., a.k.a. Snapper. (*Trouble in Paradise*) Leader of the trio of teens who torched a home belonging to a gay couple in Paradise. He provides Jesse Stone with some very helpful information about access to Stiles Island.

Jencks, Carleton, Sr. (*Trouble in Paradise*) Father of Snapper, a big, muscular man who's trying to rear his son alone.

Jennerette. (*Playmates*) Representative of the New York Federal Attorney's office; Spenser talks to him regarding a deal for Brooklyn wiseguy Bobby Deegan that involves Deegan's evidence in an off-track betting robbery and witness protection.

Jerry. (*Early Autumn*) Bartender at the New York Hilton who gives Spenser some information about Patty Giacomin.

Jessup, Tarone. (*Chance*) Henchman of crime boss Tony Marcus who runs a prostitution racket while Marcus is in prison.

Jewell. (*Perish Twice*) Tall, heroin-addicted prostitute who provides information to Sunny Randall on Gretchen Crane.

Jim. (*Perish Twice*) Bartender at Richie Burke's saloon on Portland Street.

Johnny-Behind-the-Deuce. (*Gunman's Rhapsody*) Young man about to be lynched for shooting a man.

Johnson, Major. (*Double Deuce*) Twenty-year-old leader of the Hobart Street Raiders, a gang dealing drugs.

Johnson, Mr. (*Cold Service*) Contact between Boots Podolak and the Afghani warlord who funnels heroin through him.

Johnson, Tar Baby. (*Double Play*) Big, black fighter who knocks out Joseph Burke in the ring.

Johnson, Turkey Creek Jack. (*Gunman's Rhapsody*) One of the escorts on the train carrying Morgan Earp's body to its final resting place.

Jojo. (*Playmates*) "Gunboat" of Gerry Broz.

Jones, Pat. (*Love and Glory*) General sales manager at the Discretionary Mutual Insurance Company of America.

Jourdan, Ray. (*Family Honor*) Boston University graduate student and limousine driver for Brock Patton.

Joyce, Bill. (*Gunman's Rhapsody*) Owner of the Oriental Saloon; also referred to as "Milt" and "Frank."

Joyce, Jill. (*Stardust*) One of America's most popular television stars, she's in Boston filming a new show, and she needs Spenser's protection from a stalker.

Julie. (*Family Honor, Perish Twice, Shrink Rap*) A therapist and childhood friend of Sunny Randall, she is married with a child in *Family Honor*. In *Perish Twice*, she has two children, has an affair and becomes pregnant, leaves her husband, and has an abortion. In *Shrink Rap*, she is living alone, and her husband has remarried.

Julio. (*Thin Air*) One of the muscle men working for Freddie Santiago.

Junior. (*Sudden Mischief, Family Honor, Perish Twice, Back Story, Cold Service*) Bodyguard for local crime boss Tony Marcus who is so big that, according to Hawk, "he got his own zip code" (*Sudden Mischief* 234). In *Back Story* he helps protect Spenser and Susan as a favor Marcus owes Hawk. In *Cold Service*, still working for Marcus, he's part of the operation to get rid of the Ukrainians in Marshport.

Kane, Bob. (*Poodle Springs*) L.A. plainclothes sergeant who questions Marlowe regarding Angel Victor.

Karl, Adolph. (*Wilderness*) Vicious criminal who is identified by Aaron Newman as a murderer.

Karl, Marty. (*Wilderness*) Younger son of Adolph Karl, and a member of the group with Karl when the Newmans and Hood attack.

Karl, Richie. (*Wilderness*) The older son of Adolph Karl, and a member of the group with Karl in the woods.

Karnofsky, Bonnie. (*Back Story*) See **Lombard, Bonnie**.

Karnofsky, Evelina Lombard. (*Back Story*) Mother of Bonnie and wife of Sonny who sends money every month to Barry Gordon.

Karnofsky, Sarno, a.k.a. Sonny. (*Back Story*) Crime boss who has taken over what former crime boss Joe Broz has left behind. For some reason, he seems to want Spenser to keep his nose out of the Emily Gordon case.

Kurp, Lewis, a.k.a. Mr. Shades. (*Melancholy Baby*) Lawyer and thug who beats up Sarah Markham and tells her to drop the investigation of her biological parents. Spike beats him up.

Katie. (*Valediction*) The woman with whom Hawk arranges a blind date with Spenser, to help take his mind off Susan's absence.

Katz, Doris. (*Melancholy Baby*) Attorney for Harvey Delk and July Fishbein.

Kearny. (*Sudden Mischief*) Cambridge police detective who attempts unsuccessfully to find out why Spenser and Susan were attacked by Buster DeMilo and Kenneth Philchock.

Kelly, Brian. (*Family Honor, Shrink Rap, Melancholy Baby*) In *Family Honor*, Kelly is a detective sergeant who is called to the scene when Sunny Randall shoots Terry Nee; he later dates Randall. In *Shrink Rap*, he provides information to Randall on Dr. Melvin's patients and announces that he's remarrying. In *Melancholy Baby*, he is assigned to investigate George Markham's murder. In *Death in Paradise* Jesse Stone talks to him about Gino Fish and Vinnie Morris.

Keneally, Father. (*Valediction*) Professor at Boston College and an expert on religious groups like the Reorganized Church of the Redemption; he gives Spenser some insight into the Bullies.

Kennedy, Garfield. (*Stone Cold*) Third victim of the serial killers; murder victim.

Kensey, Dr. (*The Judas Goat*) Hotel physician at the Mayfair in London who examines Spenser after an attempt on his life.

Kiernan, Faith. (*All Our Yesterdays*) Knocko Kiernan's long-suffering wife and mother of his ever-increasing brood of children.

Kiernan, Francis, a.k.a. Knocko. (*All Our Yesterdays*) Conn Sheridan's good friend and fellow Boston cop.

Kiley, Ann. (*Widow's Walk*) Good-looking attorney with Kiley & Harbaugh representing Jack DeRosa; daughter of Bobby Kiley.

Kiley, Bobby. (*Widow's Walk*) Senior partner in Kiley & Harbaugh; father of Ann Kiley.

King, Joe. (*Poodle Springs*) Producer of NDN Pictures' *Dark Adventure*.

King, Luther. (*Gunman's Rhapsody*) One of the cowboys involved in the holdup of a stagecoach.

King, Tommy. (*Trouble in Paradise*) One of the men at a poker game where Macklin rips everyone off.

Kingsley, Garrett. (*Pale Kings and Princes*) Wealthy owner and editor of the *Central Argus*, the third largest newspaper in Massachusetts. He hires Spenser to investigate the murder of his reporter Eric Valdez.

Klein, Larry. (*Hugger Mugger*) Physician for Dolly Hartman, Jason Hartman, and Walter Clive; lover of Sherry Lark.

Knox, Cynthia. (*The Widening Gyre*) One of the women involved in Gerry Broz's "granny parties." She provides information to Spenser on Gerry Broz's drug activities.

Kragan, Cathal. (*Family Honor*) Squat hit man for Rhode Island mob figure Albert Antonioni.

Kraken, Mortimer. (*Perish Twice*) Pinkie-ring-wearing boyfriend of Elizabeth Reagan who tries to blackmail her with nude photos.

Kramer, Dr. (*All Our Yesterdays*) Therapist to whom Gus Sheridan talks about the case of the child-molesting murderer.

Krueger, Elliott. (*Night Passage*) Hotshot L.A. star-maker and the man for whom Jennifer Stone has left her husband, Jesse Stone.

Ky. (*A Catskill Eagle*) Leader of the Vietnamese workers at Jerry Costigan's Pequod compound. Spenser describes him as "a pleasant snake."

Kyle, April. (*Ceremony, Taming a Sea-Horse*) Teenager on the run in *Ceremony*; she has fled from her suburban Smithfield, MA, home and its oppressive atmosphere. She would rather be a whore than go home again, and ultimately Spenser, with some input from Susan Silverman, has to make a tough decision on how best to help her. In *Taming a Sea-Horse* April has left the employ of high-class madam Patricia Utley, who hires Spenser to try to persuade April to come back to work for her. April proves obstinate, and her obstinance propels Spenser down a dark and very dangerous path to try to save her from herself.

Kyle, Bunni. (*Ceremony*) Mother of missing teenager, April Kyle; she wants her daughter back. Spenser takes the case for one dollar, since Harry Kyle refuses to pay him.

Kyle, Harry. (*Ceremony*) Father of missing teenager April Kyle, who labels his daughter a whore and doesn't want her back.

Lake, Upton. (*Shrink Rap*) Corporate counsel for Scepter Books who hires Sunny Randall as bodyguard for Melanie Joan Hall.

Lamont, Arlington. (*Stone Cold*) Name used by Anthony Lincoln; perhaps his real name.

Lamont, Mr. (*Hush Money*) Uncaring father of Prentice Lamont, who disowned his son because of his homosexuality.

Lamont, Laura. (*Hush Money*) Attractive, young second wife of Mr. Lamont.

Lamont, Patsy. (*Hush Money*) Grieving mother of Prentice Lamont.

Lamont, Prentice. (*Hush Money*) Gay graduate student at the university who recently committed suicide, allegedly over a broken affair with his professor, Robinson Nevins.

Land, Roscoe. (*Potshot*) Mayor of Potshot, AZ.

Lane, Doc. (*Trouble in Paradise, Death in Paradise*) Bartender at the Gray Gull, where Jesse Stone sometimes goes to drink. He provides some information about the Hopkins family. In *Death in Paradise* he helps the Paradise PD search for evidence in the water where the corpse is found.

Lark, Sherry. (*Hugger Mugger*) New Age ex-wife of Walter Clive and mother of Penny Clive, Stonie Wyatt, and SueSue Potter.

Larkin, Bernie. (*Perish Twice*) Detective with the Cambridge, MA, Police Department.

Laura. (*Valediction*) Woman whom Hawk is dating; he arranges a blind double date for Spenser, to help take his mind off Susan.

Leary, Mike. (*Family Honor*) Thug who attempts to shoot Sunny Randall and kidnap Millicent Patton. Randall captures him.

LeClair, Carrie, a.k.a. the Floozie. (*Shrink Rap*) Girlfriend of Richie Burke.

Lee, Fast Eddie. (*Walking Shadow*, *Chance*) Brother of Port City Theater board member Rikki Wu, Lee is head of the local Chinese crime organization and involved in smuggling illegal immigrants into the country. He is introduced in *Walking Shadow*. In *Chance*, he tells Spenser how business works among Fish, Lee, Marcus, and Ventura.

Lehman, Perry. (*Taming a Sea-Horse*) A pornographer with some powerful underworld connections, he runs a high-class men's club, the Crown Prince Club, which is a front for prostitution.

Leighton, Rowena. (*Thin Air*) Professor who teaches one of the courses Lisa St. Claire has been taking at Merrimack State College. She leads Spenser to Typhanie Hall and Luis Deleon.

LeMaster. (*Playmates*) Chief of the Taft University police.

Lenny. (*Thin Air*) Proprietor of a motorcycle repair shop in Venice, CA, from whom Spenser tries to elicit information about Angela Richard.

Leo. (*A Catskill Eagle*) Pimp killed by Spenser to protect the prostitutes Fay and Meg.

Leonard. (*Melancholy Baby, Cold Service*) Well-dressed black employee of Tony Marcus who guards Sarah Markham for Randall. In *Cold Service* he plays a major role in getting the Ukrainians out of Marshport.

Leonard O. (*Walking Shadow*) Pretentious and plagiarizing playwright of *Handy Dandy* with a voice, according to Spenser, that resembles a bleating goat.

Leong, Herman. (*Walking Shadow*) A Chinatown detective, Leong gives Spenser information on Chinese organized crime and culture in the Port City area.

Lessard, Sidney. (*Stone Cold*) One of the two boys who find the body of victim Garfield Kennedy.

Lester. (*Chance*) A friend of Hawk's from past business in Cuba, Lester operates a specialty limo service in Las Vegas.

Levesque, Roy. (*Widow's Walk*) Low-life high school boyfriend of Mary Smith.

Levine, Barry. (*All Our Yesterdays*) Butchie O'Brien's lawyer.

Levkovych, Danylko. (*Cold Service*) Member of the Ukrainian mob and one of the men with whom Hawk has a score to settle.

Lila. (*Small Vices*) Receptionist at the office across from Spenser's, she impersonates the IRS on the telephone while helping Spenser get some needed information.

Lila. (*Playmates*) Pro-Dixie Dunham waitress at the Lancaster Tap whom Spenser thinks looks like Knute Rockne.

Lincoln, Anthony, a.k.a. Tony. (*Stone Cold*) One of the suspects in the serial killings, along with his wife Brianna.

Lincoln, Brianna. (*Stone Cold*) One of the suspects in the serial killings, along with her husband Tony.

Linhares, Anton. (*Promised Land*) Assistant district attorney in New Bedford, MA.

Lipshultz, Manny, a.k.a. Lippy. (*Poodle Springs*) A casino manager just outside the city limits of Poodle Springs, he hires Marlowe to locate a photographer who skipped out on a gambling debt; murder victim.

Lister, Jermaine. (*Perish Twice*) Pimp brother of Natalie Goddard; employee of Tony Marcus.

Little, Jack. (*Mortal Stakes*) Chain-smoking PR guy for the Boston Red Sox who provides information to Spenser and introduces him to Bucky Maynard.

Livingston, Fred. (*Small Vices*) Chief of police at Pemberton College, where Melissa Henderson was killed.

Lizotti, Carmine. (*Valediction*) Cop brought to Spenser's apartment by Frank Belson, investigating Spenser's deadly encounter with a group of hit men.

Loftus, Babe. (*Stardust*) Stunt double for actress Jill Joyce; she winds up playing a role nobody wants.

Lombard, Bonnie, a.k.a. Bunny. (*Back Story*) Woman with interesting connections to the Emily Gordon murder case.

Loo, Richie. (*A Catskill Eagle*) One of the group sent by Jerry Costigan to kill Spenser and Hawk.

Loring, Brenda. (*The Godwulf Manuscript, God Save the Child, Mortal Stakes,* "Surrogate") Nubile secretary for campus security head Carl Tower who gives Spenser her phone number in *The Godwulf Manuscript.* She is mentioned as a girlfriend of Spenser's in *God Save the Child.* She's the ex-wife of Northrop May in the story "Surrogate." In *Mortal Stakes* Spenser invites her to a ball game during his investigation.

Lowell, Miriam. (*Death in Paradise*) Owner of a Dalmatian brought in to the Paradise PD.

Lucky. (*Pastime*) One of Gerry Broz's henchmen.

Lundquist, Brian P. (*Pale Kings and Princes*) Big, ambitious, pink-cheeked Massachusetts state trooper who assists Spenser with his investigation of the murder of Eric Valdez.

Lupo. (*Stardust*) Assistant Medical Examiner called to the scene of a fatal accident involving Wilfred Pomeroy.

MacCallum, Pauline, Dr. (*Paper Doll*) Headmistress of the Carolina Academy in Alton, SC, where Olivia Nelson was once a student.

Macklin, Erin. (*Double Deuce*) A former nun, she is a teacher at Marcus Garvey Middle School with the trust of the gang kids and finds Tallboy for Spenser.

Macklin, James, a.k.a. Jimmy. (*Trouble in Paradise*) Fresh out of jail, he has plans for a big score on Stiles Island.

Maguire, Earl. (*God Save the Child*) Attorney for Roger and Margery Bartlett; murder victim.

Maguire, Kevin, Detective. (*Playmates*) Brooklyn detective who provides information to Spenser on wiseguy Bobby Deegan and his involvement in a heist of a Manhattan off-track betting parlor.

Mahoney, Charley. (*Crimson Joy*) Vice cop and a patient of Susan's.

Maishe. (*Pastime*) One of Gerry Broz's henchmen.

Maitland, Bass. (*Hush Money*) Departmental ombudsman and member of the tenure committee that denied Robinson Nevins. He also appears to have a very close relationship with a fellow professor, Lillian Temple.

Malloy, Jackie. (*All Our Yesterdays*) Murdered as part of the turf war between the O'Brien gang and the Malloys.

Malloy, Kate. (*Hugger Mugger*) Red-headed, plain nanny for attorney Valerie Hatch; she claims to be being stalked by her boyfriend.

Malloy, Kevin. (*All Our Yesterdays*) Brother of Patrick Malloy.

Malloy, Patrick. (*All Our Yesterdays*) Leader of one of the Irish gangs in the South End, involved in a turf war.

Malone, Evan. (*Back Story*) FBI agent, now retired, who was in charge of the investigation into the Dread Scott Brigade and the bank robbery/murder.

Malone, Mrs. (*Back Story*) Wife of Evan Malone.

Mandy. (*Shrink Rap*) Perky assistant to Cash Resnick at Buckboard Productions.

Marc. (*Shrink Rap*) Inept young man who attempts to pick up Melanie Joan Hall in Cleveland.

Marcus, Jolene. (*Cold Service*) The troubled daughter of Tony Marcus, she's taken up with Brock Rimbaud, who fancies himself a tough guy.

Marcus, Josie. (*Gunman's Rhapsody*) Showgirl from a well-known San Francisco family and the love of Wyatt Earp's life.

Marcus, Tony. A black crime boss with a "careful" mustache (according to Spenser) who runs most of the prostitution in Boston. In *Ceremony,* Spenser has to deal with him in order to help April Kyle. In *Taming a Sea-Horse* Spenser needs help from Marcus in finding a man named Art Floyd, in his quest to find out the whereabouts of April Kyle. In *Crimson Joy* worries about the Red Rose Killer, one of whose victims was an African-American prostitute, are cutting into the prostitution gang, and Tony pledges help to Spenser and Hawk in tracking down the killer. In *Double Deuce*, he is running a drug operation in the Double Deuce area. In *Sudden Mischief*, he has been out of prison for about a year after his murder conviction in *Double Deuce*; he arranges with Spenser to set up Haskell Wechsler. In *Family Honor*, he identifies Millicent Patton's pimp for Sunny Randall and protects Randall from Cathal Kragan. In *Melancholy Baby*, he provides a thug named Leonard to watch over Sarah Markham while Randall pursues the thugs who beat up Sarah. He has some kind of deal going with the Ukrainian mob in *Cold Service*, and Spenser and Hawk have to figure out what's behind it all in order to resolve things. In *Trouble in Paradise* Crow takes the drugs he's ripped off to Marcus in order to earn some quick cash.

Margie. (*Potshot*) Cocktail waitress at the Jack Rabbit Inn who dresses like Dale Evans.

Marinaro, Phil. (*Small Vices*) Spenser's doctor when Spenser is hospitalized by an attempt on his life.

Marino, Bo. (*Stone Cold*) One of the three teenagers identified by Molly Crane as a rapist in the Candace Pennington case. He's also captain of the high school football team.

Marino, Joe. (*Stone Cold*) Father of football star Bo Marino.

Marino, Mrs. (*Stone Cold*) Mother of Bo Marino.

Markham, Barbara. (*Melancholy Baby*) Cold mother of Sarah Markham who denies that Sarah Markham is adopted.

Markham, George. (*Melancholy Baby*) Father of Sarah Markham with a background in radio and a reputation for sleeping around.

Markham, Sarah. (*Melancholy Baby*) Troubled twenty-one-year old who engages Sunny to find her birth parents.

Marlowe, Chris. (*Taming a Sea-Horse*) Pseudonym used by Spenser when he investigates the Crown Prince Club in the Caribbean.

Marlowe, Linda Potter Loring. (*Poodle Springs*) Bride of Philip Marlowe, daughter of millionaire Harlan Potter. She appeared previously in Raymond Chandler's *The Long Goodbye*.

Marlowe, Philip. (*Poodle Springs*, *Perchance to Dream*) Raymond Chandler's forty-two-year-old, tough L.A. private eye. Married to Linda Potter Loring and on the trail of deadbeat photographer Les

Valentine in *Poodle Springs*, he investigates Carmen Sternwood's disappearance in *Perchance to Dream*.

Marriott, Frank. (*Wilderness*) One of the thugs working for Adolph Karl, and a member of the group with his boss in the woods.

Mars, Eddie. (*Perchance to Dream*) Last seen as a shady casino owner who attempts to kill Philip Marlowe in Raymond Chandler's *The Big Sleep*, he is running the Cypress Club, dating Vivian Regan, and investigating Carmen Sternwood's disappearance in *Perchance to Dream*.

Martin, Hale. (*Hugger Mugger*) Trainer at the Three Fillies Stables.

Martinelli, Marty. (*Pastime*) Brother of Caitlin Moore and owner of a paving business, he gives Spenser an interesting lead in the search for Patty Giacomin.

Marty. (*Thin Air*) Hostile, unhelpful partner of Mimmi Richard.

Masterson, Bat. (*Gunman's Rhapsody*) Legendary journalist and writer.

Mastrangelo, Angelo. (*Double Play*) Bookie brother of Anthony Mastrangelo who obtains prize fights for Burke and later employs him as an enforcer for people behind on their gambling debts.

Mastrangelo, Anthony. (*Double Play*) A Marine buddy of Joseph Burke's, he introduces Burke to his brother Angelo.

Maurice. (*Double Play*) Black, muscular ex-fighter involved in a proposal to pay Jackie Robinson to play in the Negro leagues.

May, Northrop. ("Surrogate") Impotent ex-husband of Brenda Loring.

Maynard, Bucky. (*Mortal Stakes*) Described by Spenser as "a man with several chins" (*Mortal Stakes* 32), he is announcer for the Boston Red Sox, and a man with a lot of power. Jack Little advises Spenser to tread lightly around him and his pretty-boy bodyguard, Lester Floyd.

McBride, Debbie. (*All Our Yesterdays*) Girl Scout injured because of the gang fighting in the South End.

McCafferty. (*Valediction*) Thoracic surgeon who works on Spenser after he gets hit in the chest by two bullets.

McCallister, Adele. (*Bad Business*) A "flamboyantly good-looking" woman who works at Kinergy and who is the first to blow the whistle on the strange goings-on.

McCann, Denny. (*Gunman's Rhapsody*) Man involved in a bar fight with Ike Clanton, who challenges him to a duel on Allen Street.

McCann, Sawyer. (*Back Story*) Black activist (Hawk calls him "the last hippie") who fills in Spenser and Hawk on the origins of the Dread Scott Brigade and its members.

McDermott, Margaret. (*Widow's Walk*) Girlfriend of Jack DeRosa; murder victim.

McDermott, Rich. (*Promised Land*) Police detective in New Bedford, MA.

McGonigle, J. T. (*Trouble in Paradise*) Security man working at the entrance to Stiles Island. Macklin and his gang kill him in their scheme to take over the island.

McGonigle, Kevin. (*Widow's Walk*) Thug who attempts to shoot Spenser; associate of Jack DeRosa; murder victim.

McKean, Kodi. (*Cold Service*) Name being used by the Gray Man, a.k.a. Rugar.

McKinnon. (*A Catskill Eagle*) FBI agent who deals with Ives, Quirk, Spenser, and Hawk to get the charges dropped against Spenser and Hawk in exchange for killing Jerry Costigan.

McLaury, Frank. (*Gunman's Rhapsody*) Rancher accused of the theft of Army mules.

McLaury, Tom. (*Gunman's Rhapsody*) Brother of Frank.

McMahon. (*Valediction*) Scruffy narcotics cop from Quincy who assists on the case against Paultz Construction Company.

McMartin, Glenda Baker. (*Small Vices*) One of the students at Pemberton College who was a witness to Melissa Henderson's abduction. She is now married to Hunt McMartin.

McMartin, Hunt. (*Small Vices*) One of the students at Pemberton College who was a witness to Melissa Henderson's abduction. Now married to Glenda Baker McMartin, he also has a family connection to another person involved in the case.

McMasters, Sherman. (*Gunman's Rhapsody*) One of the escorts for the transport of Morgan Earp's body.

McNeeley, Millie. (*Melancholy Baby*) Long-time employee of Moline, IL, talk radio station WMOL; former coworker of George Markham. She provides Sunny Randall with information about George Markham's past.

McNeely, Tom. (*Ceremony*) Boston vice squad cop to whom Spenser goes with his plan to bring down a teenage pornography ring.

McPhail, Georgie. (*Family Honor*) Muscle for Cathal Kragan. Spike beats him up.

Meehan, Bucko. (*Family Honor*) Fat extortion specialist in Boston who sends Terry Nee and Mike Leary to shoot Sunny Randall and kidnap Millicent Patton; murder victim.

Meeker, Anthony, a.k.a. Tony the Phony. (*Chance*) A compulsive gambler and serial cheater, he is the son-in-law of and bagman for crime boss Julius Ventura. Spenser is hired to find him.

Meeker, Shirley. (*Chance*) Pudgy and emotionally crippled daughter of crime boss Julius Ventura and wife of Anthony Meeker; rape and murder victim.

Meg. (*A Catskill Eagle*) Blonde, olive-skinned prostitute; Spenser and Hawk take refuge in her San Francisco apartment after Spenser breaks Hawk out of jail.

Mei Ling, a.k.a. Missy. (*Walking Shadow, Chance*) Small-boned, excessively polite Harvard graduate student in Asian Studies originally from Taipei. In *Walking Shadow* and *Chance*, she serves as a translator for Spenser and seems fascinated by Hawk.

Melvin, John. (*Shrink Rap*) Psychiatrist ex-husband and stalker of Melanie Joan Hall.

Merchant, Bob. (*Night Passage*) Father of Michelle and a member of Freedom's Horsemen. The group assembles in his carriage house before their assault on Jesse Stone and the Paradise PD.

Merchant, Michelle. (*Night Passage*) Teenager who spends a lot of time smoking dope. Jesse Stone starts talking to her, and eventually she acts to help him in a significant way.

Merchent, Jennifer Grayle. (*Love and Glory*) Object of Boone Adams's obsession at Colby College, she marries John Merchent and later re-meets Adams at Taft University where she is a teaching assistant.

Merchent, John. (*Love and Glory*) Self-important Cornell graduate who marries Jennifer Grayle; later becomes an English professor at Taft University.

Merchent, Margaret. (*Love and Glory*) Bossy and alcoholic mother of John Merchent.

Merchent, Suzanna, a.k.a. Sue-Sue. (*Love and Glory*) Petulant five-and-a-half-year-old daughter of John and Jennifer Merchent.

Merriam, June. (*Playmates*) Trim, proper secretary to Taft University president Adrian Cort, she provides Dwayne Woodcock's transcript and other information to Spenser and is unamused by him.

Meyer, Norman. (*Shrink Rap*) State police detective investigating Kim Crawford's death; former colleague of Phil Randall.

Michael. (*Family Honor*) Spouse of Sunny Randall's friend Julie.

Michelle. (*Ceremony*) One of the girls hanging out with Hummer; she gives Spenser a lead to April Kyle.

Mickey. (*Ceremony*) Bouncer at Mitch Poitras's house who can't cope with Hawk and Spenser.

Mikey. (*Family Honor*) Six-year-old son of Sunny Randall's friend Julie.

Mikkleson, Bob. (*Stone Cold*) Manager of the television station where Jennifer Stone is working as "weather girl." Jesse Stone confronts Jennifer and Bob outside the station.

Milford, Iris. (*The Godwulf Manuscript*) Fat, black single mother and feature editor for the university newspaper. She provides Spenser with information during his investigation of the Powell murder. She also is mentioned in *Double Deuce* as having told Erin Macklin that Spenser can leap tall buildings in a single bound (*Double Deuce* 86).

Miller, Tommy. (*Small Vices*) Massachusetts State Police detective who investigated the murder of Pemberton College student Melissa Henderson. He's not happy that Spenser is questioning the investigation.

Millicent. (*Double Play*) An unbalanced fan who wants a rendezvous with Jackie Robinson.

Mills, Maggie. (*Widow's Walk*) Attorney for Amy Peters.

Millwood, Sally. (*Shrink Rap*) Patient of John Melvin's; murder victim.

Milo. (*The Judas Goat*) One of the terrorists found dead in Amsterdam by Hawk and Spenser.

Milo, Mr. (*Taming a Sea-Horse*) Underworld figure who tries to have Spenser killed because Spenser refuses to leave Perry Lehman alone.

Miranda. (*Melancholy Baby*) Tactful manager at Spike's restaurant.

Mister Bubbles. (*Family Honor*) A clown with a lousy attitude with children.

Monson. (*Poodle Springs*) Young cop from the Poodle Springs police department.

Montana, Lou. (*Walking Shadow*) Portly director of *Handy Dandy*, the play performed at the Port City Theater Company.

Montenegro, Franco. (*A Savage Place*) Fat henchman of Oceania Industries executive Peter Brewster. He beats up TV reporter Candy Sloan and is later shot by Rollie Simms, Brewster's chief of security.

Monforte, Lola. (*Perchance to Dream*) An actress and former resident of Resthaven; murder victim.

Moore, Caitlin. (*Pastime*) Best friend of Patty Giacomin, she gives Spenser and Paul some information in their quest to track down the missing woman.

Morales, Esther. (*Widow's Walk*) Cleaning woman for Mary and Nathan Smith who provides information to Spenser on their married life.

Morgan. (*The Judas Goat*) Officer of the Royal Canadian Mounted Police who questions Spenser and Hawk after their confrontation with Paul and Zachary at the Montreal Olympic Games.

Morgan, Maxwell T. (*Hush Money*) Broker at Hall, Peary who handles the account set up by Prentice Lamont.

Moriarty, Arthur. (*God Save the Child*) Assistant principal of Smithfield's high school.

Morris, Vinnie. In *The Widening Gyre*, right-hand man for mobster Joe Broz. In *Valediction* Spenser calls him for information on the Paultz Construction Company, which he suspects is using the Reorganized Church of the Redemption to launder drug money. In *Pastime* Morris lets Spenser know that Joe Broz's son, Gerry, is looking for Rich Beaumont and why. Eventually he has to decide whether to hang around while the ageing Broz decides whether he'll let his inept son take over the business. In *Walking Shadow*, he has retired and, bored, comes along as backup for Hawk and Spenser when they go to Port City. In *Chance* and *Small*

Vices, now working as a bodyguard for Gino Fish, he's still willing to lend Spenser a hand. In *Potshot*, he joins Spenser's posse to rid Potshot, AZ, of the gang called the Dell. In *Widow's Walk*, he tails Marvin Conroy and Ann Kiley. He helps Spenser identify a hired gun who comes calling in his office, warning Spencer off the Emily Gordon case, in *Back Story*. In *Bad Business* Spenser asks him to guard Adele McCallister after she decides to blow the whistle on Kinergy. In *Night Passage* he's in the office with Gino Fish when Jo Jo Genest comes to call. In *Death in Paradise* Jesse Stone talks to him about Elinor Bishop when he visits Gino's office, but Vinnie knows nothing about the dead girl.

Morrissey, Ray. (*Stardust*) Boston cop assigned to watch over actress Jill Joyce.

Morton, Barton. (*Playmates*) Chairman of the Board of Trustees of Taft University, he hires Spenser on behalf of the board to investigate charges of point shaving by the basketball team.

Mulready, Michael. (*Looking for Rachel Wallace*) Hapless cousin of Mingo Mulready who with Swisher Cody attempts to run Spenser off the road. Spenser strands him in Milton.

Mulready, Mingo. (*Looking for Rachel Wallace*) Part-time driver and full-time muscle for Mrs. English.

Murphy. (*Thin Air*) A cop in Proctor.

Murphy, Billy. (*Love and Glory*) Classmate of Boone Adams at Colby College.

Murphy, Madeline. (*Double Play*) A fat young nurse who takes care of wounded veteran Joseph Burke once he has been released from the hospital.

Murphy, Polly. (*Melancholy Baby*) Childhood friend and former roommate of Sarah Markham at Taft University. She tells Randall about Sarah's life as a party girl.

Nancy. (*Pastime*) One of Patty Giacomin's coworkers at the realty company.

Nee, Terry. (*Family Honor*) Thug who works for Bucko Meehan and attempts to shoot Sunny Randall and kidnap Millicent Patton; murder victim.

Nelson, Jack. (*Paper Doll*) Elderly father of Olivia Nelson, he is not much help to Spenser.

Nelson, Olivia. (*Paper Doll*) The murdered wife of prominent businessman Loudon Tripp; she was seemingly the perfect wife and mother, yet someone murdered her in a brutal fashion.

Nevins, Bobby. (*Hush Money*) Trainer and former mentor of Hawk, he is also the father of Robinson Nevins and the reason that Hawk involves Spenser in the case.

Nevins, Robinson. (*Hush Money*) Professor of English at a university (Harvard) who hires Spenser to find out what was behind the campaign to keep him from getting tenure.

Newman, Aaron. (*Wilderness*) Successful writer who witnesses a murder while out for a jog one morning; after his wife is threatened by thugs, he must decide how to resolve the situation.

Newman, Janet. (*Wilderness*) Wife of Aaron Newman; after she is assaulted and threatened by thugs, she encourages her husband to resolve the situation by killing the man who has threatened them.

Nogarian, Milo. (*Stardust*) Executive producer of the television show starring volatile actress Jill Joyce.

Nolan, Louis. (*The Widening Gyre*) Worker for Vinnie Morris who hires Pelletier and Ricci to rough up Meade Alexander's campaign workers.

Noon, Tommy. (*Melancholy Baby*) A hired gun who shoots George Markham.

Norris, Vincent. (*Perchance to Dream*) Butler for the late General Sternwood and Vivian Regan, he hires Marlowe to find the missing Carmen Sternwood.

North, Shirley. (*Looking for Rachel Wallace*) Chain-smoking blonde host of the TV show *Contact*. She interviews Rachel Wallace.

Nuncio. (*Cold Service*) One of the men working for Brock Rimbaud.

O'Brien, Bobby. (*Melancholy Baby*) Hockey-playing former high school boyfriend of Sarah Markham with a rust-colored crew cut. He tells Randall about Sarah Markham's difficult past.

O'Brien, Butchie. (*All Our Yesterdays*) Tavern owner, leader of one of the Irish gangs in the South End, and an old friend of Gus Sheridan's.

O'Brien, Corky. (*All Our Yesterdays*) Brother of Butchie O'Brien; his murder touches off a turf war in the South End.

O'Connor. (*Hush Money*) Police sergeant in Reading to whom Spenser speaks about keeping an eye on KC Roth and her alleged stalker.

O'Dell, Reilly. (*Paper Doll*) An employee of a Washington, D.C.–based security firm, he's one of the men who tries to convince Spenser to back off the case in Alton, SC.

O'Gorman, Seamus. (*All Our Yesterdays*) One of Conn Sheridan's fellow IRA captains in Ireland; an Australian Irishman.

Ohls, Bernie, Lieutenant. (*Poodle Springs, Perchance to Dream*) Cigar-chomping chief investigator for the L.A. district attorney assigned to the Lola Faithful case in *Poodle Springs* and the investigation of a dismembered corpse in *Perchance to Dream*.

Old Gunner. (*All Our Yesterdays*) One of Conn Sheridan's fellow prisoners in Kilmainham jail.

Olmo, Juanita. (*Pale Kings and Princes*) Social worker at the Wheaton Union Hospital. She tells Spenser that Eric Valdez was sleeping with Emmy Esteva.

O'Mara, Darrin. (*Bad Business*) Charismatic radio personality who espouses some interesting ideas on courtly love for the modern world.

O'Neill, Elmer. (*Bad Business*) Private detective who is tailing Ellen Eisen because her husband, Bernard Eisen, suspects she's cheating on him.

Ong, Mr. and Mrs. (*Walking Shadow*) Owners of a Chinese medicine shop in Port City. Spenser is ambushed outside of their shop by members of the Death Dragons.

Orchard, Roland. (*The Godwulf Manuscript*) Wealthy, heavy-drinking father of Terry Orchard; senior partner of Orchard, Bonner and Blanch. He hires Spenser to clear his daughter of the charge of murdering her boyfriend Dennis Powell.

Orchard, Marion. (*The Godwulf Manuscript*) Wealthy and bored mother of Terry Orchard. She sleeps with Spenser.

Orchard, Terry. (*The Godwulf Manuscript*) Secretary of SCACE (Student Committee Against Capitalist Exploitation) and Spenser's client, accused of murdering her boyfriend Dennis Powell.

Otis, Elinor, a.k.a. Billie. (*Family Honor*) Brock and Betty Patton's maid. She provides information to Sunny Randall on the Pattons.

Otis, John. (*Family Honor*) Butler to Brock and Betty Patton. He provides information to Sunny Randall on the Pattons.

Owens, Bob. (*Valediction*) Director of Community Relations for the Reorganized Church of the Redemption.

Owens, Richard. (*Stone Cold*) One of the two boys who find the body of murder victim Garfield Kennedy.

Paglia, Gennaro, a.k.a. Johnny. (*Double Play*) Mobster owner of a Harlem restaurant, he has a confrontation with Jackie Robinson and Joseph Burke.

Paige. (*Valediction*) Girlfriend of Paul Giacomin. She's also a dancer.

Parisi, Bruce. (*Small Vices*) Owner of a maroon station wagon, which a group of four hired guns drove when they came to Spenser's office on an intimidation call. Spenser convinces him to come across with information he needs.

Parker, Peter. (*Small Vices*) Alias Spenser uses with a young woman in the press office at Taft University when he asks for information on Clint Stapleton.

Patterson, Frank. (*Gunman's Rhapsody*) Neighbor of rancher Frank McLaury.

Patton, Betty. (*Family Honor*) Unfaithful wife of Brock Patton; mother of Millicent.

Patton, Brock. (*Family Honor*) Philandering CEO of the bank MassBay Trust and Massachusetts gubernatorial hopeful who hires Sunny Randall to find his missing daughter.

Patton, Millicent, a.k.a. Millie. (*Family Honor*) The Pattons' missing fifteen-year-old daughter.

Paul. (*The Judas Goat*) Terrorist at the head of the group Liberty, which aims restore the white race to power in Africa.

Paul, Bob. (*Gunman's Rhapsody*) Shotgun messenger on the stagecoach.

Paulie. (*Stardust*) Driver for actress Jill Joyce.

Paultz, Mickey. (*Valediction*) Owner of the Paultz Construction Company. Spenser suspects that the company is using the Reorganized Church of the Redemption to launder drug money.

Pearl, a.k.a the Wonder Dog. (*Pastime, Back Story*) Solid chocolate German shorthair pointer, renamed by Spenser, who becomes the canine companion of Spenser and Susan from this book on. Susan's ex-husband leaves Pearl with her when he moves to England. In *Back Story*, the original Pearl has died, and Spenser goes to Toronto to pick up a fifteen-month-old solid chocolate German shorthair pointer, named Robin Hood's Purple Sandpiper. Spenser and Susan call her Pearl.

Pelletier, Sal. (*The Widening Gyre*) Tattooed tough who roughs up Meade Alexander's campaign workers until Spenser steps in.

Pennington, Candace. (*Stone Cold*) Teenager who comes to Jesse Stone's office with her mother, claiming she was raped.

Pennington, Chuck. (*Stone Cold*) An architect and father of rape victim Candace Pennington.

Pennington, Margaret. (*Stone Cold*) Mother of Candace Pennington, rape victim.

Pepe. (*Family Honor*) A bored pony.

Perkins, Peter. (*Night Passage, Trouble in Paradise, Death in Paradise, Stone Cold*) Crime scene specialist for the Paradise PD. He appears in this capacity in all the Jesse Stone books and in his role as a patrol officer as well.

Peters, Amy. (*Widow's Walk*) Vice-president for public affairs at Pequod Savings & Loan who talks to Spenser regarding Nathan Smith; murder victim.

Petrocelli, Nick. (*Trouble in Paradise*) New town counsel for Paradise who has succeeded Abby Taylor.

Pettler, R. J., a.k.a. Dick. (*Death in Paradise*) Private detective hired by Felicia Shaw's lawyer to get the dirt on Norman Shaw.

Phil. (*The Godwulf Manuscript*) Thug of crime boss Joe Broz. He attempts to kill Spenser.

Philchock, Kenneth, a.k.a. Shorty. (*Sudden Mischief*) Short, sharp-nosed bodyguard for loanshark Haskell Wechsler.

Phillies, Philadelphia. (*Double Play*) The 1947 Philadelphia Phillies roster that played against the Brooklyn Dodgers was composed of Del Ennis (left field), Charlie Gilbert (outfielder, pinch hitter), Dutch Leonard (pitcher), Skeeter Newsome (shortstop), Charley Schanz (pitcher), Howie Schultz (first base), Andy Seminick (catcher), Jim Tabor (third base), Emil Verban (second base), Harry Walker (centerfield), and Johnny Wyrostek (right field).

Phillips, Buford L. (*Stardust*) Chief of Police in Waymark, MA, where Spenser tracks down Wilfred Pomeroy. Spenser later has a bone to pick with Chief Phillips.

Philpot, Bud. (*Gunman's Rhapsody*) Stagecoach driver for Wells Fargo; later killed during a robbery.

Piper, Winston. (*All Our Yesterdays*) Mayor who succeeds Parnell Flaherty.

Pirates, Pittsburgh. (*Double Play*) The 1947 Pittsburgh Pirates roster that played against the Brooklyn Dodgers was composed of Jimmy Bloodworth (second base), Tiny Bonham (pitcher), Billy Cox (shortstop), Hank Greenberg (first base), Frankie Gustine (third base), Kirby Higbe (pitcher), Dixie Howell (catcher), Ralph Kiner (left field), Clyde Kluttz (catcher), Culley Rikard (right field), Jim Russell (centerfield), Bill Salkeld (catcher, pinch hitter), and Elmer Singleton (pitcher).

Plante, Mr. (*A Catskill Eagle*) "Cadre chief" of the mercenary camp run by Jerry Costigan.

Ploughman, Matthew. (*Night Passage*) Man questioned in Wyoming concerning the death of former Paradise Chief of Police Tom Carson.

Plum, Pauline. (*Family Honor*) Head of the Pinkett School, where Millicent Patton is enrolled.

Podolak, Boots. (*Cold Service*) The mayor of Marshport, he's also head of the Ukrainian mob trying to move into Tony Marcus's territory.

Poitras, Mitchell. (*Ceremony*) A colleague of Susan Silverman's; with an important job as Executive Coordinator of the Student Guidance and Counseling Administration in Massachusetts, he seems to have an unusual interest in sex, teenagers, and pornography; Amy Gurwitz lives with him in Back Bay Boston.

Pollinger, T. P. (*Death in Paradise*) One of the clients of the services provided by Alan Garner.

Pomeroy, Wilfred. (*Stardust*) Sad, ineffectual man with connections to actress Jill Joyce's past.

Pontevecchio, Elwood, a.k.a. Woody. (*Thin Air*) An old friend of Angela Richard and once her pimp, he now fancies himself as a hotshot producer in L.A.

Pony. (*Potshot*) Long-haired goon for the Preacher who threatened Steve Buckman.

Pope, Daryl. (*Playmates*) Reserve forward for the Taft University basketball team.

Porter, John. (*Double Deuce*) A bodybuilder type and member of the Hobart Street Raiders. Hawk decks him with one punch and later shoots him in the shoulder.

Portugal, Bobby. (*Night Passage*) Self-described "loser" husband of murder victim Tammy Portugal.

Portugal, Tammy. (*Night Passage*) Girlfriend of Hasty Hathway who becomes a problem that can be solved only by murder.

Potter, Pud. (*Hugger Mugger*) Alcoholic son-in-law of Walter Clive who attempts, unsuccessfully, to punch Spenser.

Potter, SueSue. (*Hugger Mugger*) Alcoholic daughter of Walter Clive who makes a pass at Spenser.

Powell, Dennis. (*The Godwulf Manuscript*) Belligerent, possessive boyfriend of Terry Orchard; drug dealer; murder victim.

Powers, King. (*Promised Land*) Loanshark who wants his money from the tardy Harv Spenser and has a wardrobe that is "Robert Hall Mod."

Preacher. (*Potshot*) Hairless leader of the gang called the Dell in Potshot, AZ, shaking down the town for protection money.

Pritchard, Sybil. (*Back Story*) Sister of murder victim Emily Gordon and aunt of Daryl Silver.

Prohorovych, Lyaksandro. (*Cold Service*) Member of the Ukrainian mob and one of the men with whom Hawk has a score to settle.

Pryor. (*Widow's Walk*) Youth service officer for the town of Franklin who provides information to Spenser on Mary Smith's high school friends.

Putnam, Penny. (*Sudden Mischief*) A volunteer for Galapalooza and one of the plaintiffs in the sexual harassment suit against Brad Sterling.

Quagliozzi, Carla. (*Sudden Mischief*) President of the bogus charity Civil Streets and an ex-wife of Brad Sterling; murder victim.

Quant, Milo. (*Hush Money*) Charismatic leader of the "Last Stand" movement, which wants to alert people to the supposed threat posed to American civilization by blacks, Jews, and homosexuals.

Quentin, Nancy. (*Valediction*) Dance critic at the *Boston Globe* who gives Spenser information on Tommy Banks and his company.

Quince, Ms. (*Crimson Joy*) One of a group who confronts Martin Quirk over its concerns over the investigation into the Red Rose killings.

Quinn, Marge. (*Perish Twice*) Employee of the motor vehicles registry.

Quinton. (*Double Deuce*) One of Erin Macklin's students.

Quirk, Martin. Sharply dressed commander of the Boston homicide bureau. In *The Godwulf Manuscript* he is in charge of the Powell case. In *God Save the Child*, he provides information on Dr. Croft to Spenser. In *Mortal Stakes* Spenser consults him in his attempt to find a solution to the dilemma facing Marty and Linda Rabb. In *Looking for Rachel Wallace*, he and Spenser consult about Wallace's kidnapping. In *Ceremony* he appears briefly with Frank Belson when Spenser needs backup while confronting a dangerous businessman. In *The Widening Gyre*, he gives Spenser the file on Joe Broz from the police's Organized Crime Unit. In *Valediction* he gives Spenser a lead to an expert on religious cults. He's also in on the case against the Paultz Construction Company. In *A Catskill Eagle*, he accuses Spenser of violating "the entire California penal code"; acts as a go-between for Spenser, Hawk, the FBI, and the CIA; and moves Susan and Rachel Wallace to a safe place. In *Double Deuce*, he trips Tony Marcus's bodyguard and arrests Marcus. In *Paper Doll* he comes to Alton, SC, to get Spenser out of trouble when the local police (with some outside help) start leaning on him. In *Playmates*, he hosts Spenser, Belson, Middlesex County DA Arlett, Taft University police chief LeMaster, and Walford cop Stuart Delaney to discuss the murder of Taft basketball player Danny Davis. In *Walking Shadow*, he refers Spenser to Herman Leong, a Chinatown detective. In *Thin Air* he talks to Spenser about Frank Belson and his second wife, Lisa St. Claire, giving Spenser some helpful background information. In *Sudden Mischief*, Quirk has been promoted to captain and is assigned to investigate the corpse found by Spenser and Hawk in Brad Sterling's office. In *Hugger Mugger*, he provides information to Spenser on Jon Delroy. In *Widow's Walk*, Spenser consults with him on Nathan Smith's murder. In *Back Story* he helps Spenser with information on the Dread Scott Brigade and the bank robbery during which Daryl Silver's mother was murdered twenty-eight years before. He's investigating a murder tied into Spenser's case at Kinergy in *Bad Business*.

Rabb, Linda. (*Mortal Stakes*) Beautiful wife of Boston Red Sox pitcher Marty Rabb and mother of Marty Jr. Spenser suspects that Marty Sr.'s problems may lie somewhere in his wife's past.

Rabb, Marty. (*Mortal Stakes*) Talented young pitcher with the Boston Red Sox suspected of fixing games. Spenser delves into his life and that of Rabb's wife, Linda.

Race. (*Perchance to Dream*) Thug for Dr. Bonsentir who resembles a California beachboy; Lieutenant Bernie Ohls throws him into a fireplace.

Race, Hal. (*Shrink Rap*) Egotistical actor interested in starring in a film of Melanie Joan Hall's books.

Rackley. (*Perchance to Dream*) A Long Beach, CA, police captain.

Rafferty. (*All Our Yesterdays*) Boston homicide cop who finds a young murder victim and calls Gus Sheridan to the scene.

Rafferty, Mickey. (*A Savage Place*) Pint-sized stuntman and sometime boyfriend of TV reporter Candy Sloan who witnesses a mob payoff from a producer and is later killed.

Raines, Jackie. (*Double Deuce*) A stunning producer for the Marge Eagen Show, she is gathering material for a program on Boston gangs and is Hawk's latest girlfriend.

Rambeaux, Robert. (*Taming a Sea-Horse*) Pimp with a musical bent (he's actually enrolled in classes at Juilliard) who has taken April Kyle away from her job with Patricia Utley. When he is murdered, Spenser seeks his killer in order to determine the whereabouts of April Kyle.

Randall. (*Stardust*) Hired muscle working for Stanley Rojack, who comes off second-best to Spenser.

Randall, Em. (*Family Honor*) Disapproving mother of Sunny Randall and Elizabeth Reagan.

Randall, Phil. (*Family Honor, Melancholy Baby*) Retired cop and indulgent father of daughters Sunny Randall and Elizabeth Reagan. In *Melancholy Baby*, he tracks down the address of Ike Rosen via his police connections and provides advice to Randall regarding the Sarah Markham case.

Randall, Sonya, a.k.a. Sunny. (*Family Honor, Perish Twice, Shrink Rap, Melancholy Baby*) Five-foot-six ex-cop turned PI, blonde, one-hundred-fifteen pounds. Artist and ex-wife of tavern owner Richie Burke.

Randall, Travis, Lieutenant. (*Trouble in Paradise*) Sheriff's deputy in Pima County, AZ, and an old friend of Jesse Stone and his family. Stone calls him, seeking information on Wilson Cromartie, a.k.a. Crow.

Randolph, Rich. (*Hush Money*) Television reporter who was a target of the outing campaign led by Prentice Lamont.

Rankin, Bertha Voss. (*Paper Doll*) Mother of Cheryl Anne Rankin.

Rankin, Cheryl Anne. (*Paper Doll*) A young woman who looks remarkably like Olivia Nelson; Spenser spots an old photograph of her in Alton, SC.

Raphael, Estelle. (*Widow's Walk*) Hawk's girlfriend and a doctor who runs a fertility clinic in Brookline, MA.

Rashad, Representative. (*Crimson Joy*) One of a group who comes to air its concerns with Martin Quirk over the conduct of the investigation into the Red Rose killings.

Ratliff, Mark. (*Potshot*) A movie producer in Potshot, AZ, with ties to Mary Lou Buckman.

Ratliff, Nancy. (*Potshot*) Bitter ex-wife of Mark Ratliff.

Reagan, Elizabeth Randall. (*Perish Twice*) Sunny's judgmental sister. In *Perish Twice*, she asks Sunny to find out if her husband is cheating on her.

Reagan, Hal. (*Perish Twice*) Elizabeth Randall's cheating husband and a lawyer at Cone Oakes.

Reagan, Henry. (*Love and Glory*) L.A. carpenter who employs Boone Adams as an assistant.

Reagan, Martin. (*Stone Cold*) An Essex County, MA, assistant DA.

Reardon, Bill. (*Love and Glory*) Boone Adams's superior and director of advertising, public relations, and sales promotion at the Discretionary Mutual Insurance Company of America.

Rebello, Ms. (*Walking Shadow*) Limping landlady of actor Craig Sampson.

Red. (*A Catskill Eagle*) Chatty mercenary for hire for Jerry Costigan; fond of arm wrestling.

Red. (*Ceremony*) Pimp for whom April Kyle has been working; he seems very determined to keep Spenser away from April.

Redfield, Len. (*Gunman's Rhapsody*) Owner of a ranch where some men on the run are suspected of hiding.

Reds, Cincinnati. (*Double Play*) The 1947 Cincinnati Reds roster that played against the Brooklyn Dodgers was composed of Bobby Adams (second base), Frank Baumholtz (right field), Joe Beggs (pitcher), Augie Galen (outfielder), Harry Gumbert (pitcher), Bert Haas (first base, outfielder), Grady Hatton (third base), Eddie Lukon (left field), Eddie Miller (shortstop), Ray Mueller (catcher), Clyde Shoun (pitcher), Tommy Tatum (centerfield), Johnny Vander Meer (pitcher), Clyde Vollmer (left field), Bucky Walters (pitcher), and Babe Young (first base).

Reenie. (*Love and Glory*) Bartender at Onie's bar near Colby College.

Reeves, Lawrence B. (*Perish Twice*) Stalker of Mary Lou Goddard; murder victim.

Regan, Vivian Sternwood. (*Perchance to Dream*) Beautiful wife of murder victim Rusty Regan and daughter of General Sternwood in Chandler's *The Big Sleep*, she has a yen for Marlowe, dates casino owner Eddie Mars, and has to care for her younger sister Carmen in *Perchance to Dream*.

Reilly, Sean. (*Sudden Mischief*) Spenser's on-call computer geek with a patchy beard, not known for his fashion sense and given to carrying a black plastic briefcase. He finds Brad Sterling's unlisted phone number for Spenser and unlocks files on Sterling's computer disks.

Remmert, Linda. (*The Widening Gyre*) Sixteen-year-old girl who smuggles Spenser into one of Gerry Broz's "granny parties."

Resnick, Cash. (*Shrink Rap*) A bored young producer at Buckboard Productions.

Resnick, Sheldon. (*Stone Cold*) Lawyer retained by the parents of Candace Pennington.

Reston, Claire. (*Small Vices*) Restless wife who invites Hawk to join her in her room while her husband is occupied elsewhere.

Reynolds. (*Hush Money*) Dean of the School of Arts and Sciences at the university, from whom Spenser gains access to Prentice Lamont's transcript, among other things.

Ricardo, Sondra Lee. (*Poodle Springs*) Frisky, alcoholic model with some compromising photographs in her past.

Ricardo, Tommy. (*Poodle Springs*) Jealous husband of Sondra Lee.

Ricci, Pat. (*The Widening Gyre*) Gray-haired thug who roughs up two college-age campaign workers for Meade Alexander.

Rice, Billy. (*Hugger Mugger*) Groom at Three Fillies Stables.

Richard. (*Double Play*) Unsuccessful would-be assassin of Jackie Robinson.

Richard, Angela. (*Thin Air*) Former name of Lisa St. Claire.

Richard, Lawrence Vaughn. (*Thin Air*) Father of Angela Richard.

Richard, Mimmi. (*Thin Air*) The mother of Angela Richard who wants nothing to do with her wayward daughter.

Richards, Beaumont. (*Pastime*) Pseudonym used by Rich Beaumont in his attempt to hide from Gerry Broz.

Rickey, Branch. ("Harlem Nocturne," *Double Play*) The Brooklyn Dodgers general manager who was responsible for bringing Jackie Robinson to the major leagues and ending its prohibition against players of color. In "Harlem Nocturne," he hires the unnamed narrator to protect Robinson. In *Double Play*, he hires Joseph Burke to guard Robinson.

Riggs, Marty. (*Stardust*) Executive from Zenith Meridien Television, the studio which is producing Jill Joyce's television series in Boston.

Rimbaud, Brock. (*Cold Service*) Living with Jolene Marcus, he thinks he's tough enough to play in the same league as Tony Marcus and the Ukrainians.

Ringo, Johnny. (*Gunman's Rhapsody*) Cowboy and a friend of Curley Bill Brocius.

Riordan. (*Valediction*) "Large mean" ATF cop who assists on the case against Paultz Construction Company.

Rita. (*Perchance to Dream*) Dim, gum-cracking receptionist for Rancho Springs Development Corporation.

Ritchie. (*Early Autumn*) Assistant Manager at the New York Hilton who gives Spenser some interesting information about Patty Giacomin.

Rittenhouse, Agnes. (*A Savage Place*) Plump publicist for Summit Studios with a yen for Spenser.

Roach. (*Hush Money*) Chief of police in Hingham, MA, where Louis Vincent lives.

Roach, Julius. (*Double Play*) A shady political bigwig, he hires Joseph Burke to guard his daughter Lauren.

Roach, Lauren. (*Double Play*) The troubled, violet-eyed daughter of Julius Roach; she is involved with Louis Boucicault, the son of a gangster, and falls in love with Joseph Burke.

Roach, Mrs. (*Double Play*) Alcoholic wife of Julius Roach.

Robert. (*Perish Twice*) Bearded boyfriend of Sunny Randall's friend Julie.

Robinson, Jack Roosevelt, a.k.a. Jackie. ("Harlem Nocturne," *Double Play*) Legendary first baseman who broke the major leagues' color barrier in 1947. In "Harlem Nocturne" and *Double Play*, his life is threatened and he has a showdown with a mob bigwig.

Robinson, Kendall. (*All Our Yesterdays*) Suffolk County, MA, DA.

Robinson, Rachel. (*Double Play*) Wife of Jackie Robinson.

Rocco, a.k.a. Rock. (*Pastime*) Bartender of a joint where Spenser goes to meet Gerry Broz.

Rocky. (*A Catskill Eagle*) A fleshy security guard at Jerry Costigan's estate.

Rodriguez, Arlene. (*Double Deuce*) Caseworker for the Department of Youth Services who provides information to Spenser on Major Johnson's juvenile arrest record.

Rogers, Bailey. (*Pale Kings and Princes*) Red-faced, fat-necked police chief in Wheaton who stonewalls Spenser regarding the murder of Eric Valdez; murder victim.

Rogers, Brett. (*Pale Kings and Princes*) Seventeen-year-old, overweight, mentally slow son of Bailey and Caroline Rogers; employed as a driver by Felipe Esteva; murder victim.

Rogers, Caroline. (*Pale Kings and Princes*) Librarian wife of Bailey Rogers.

Rojack, Stanley. (*Stardust*) Hard-nosed businessman with powerful connections, who has been spurned by actress Jill Joyce; he doesn't want to take "no" for an answer.

Romero. (*Chance*) Leathery detective sergeant with Las Vegas homicide who is assigned to Shirley Meeker's murder.

Romero, Ben. (*Night Passage*) Jesse Stone's partner in the LAPD, who tells Stone he won't work with him any longer because of Stone's drinking.

Ronan, Francis. (*Sudden Mischief*) A Taft University law professor and former judge, he files a sexual harassment suit against Brad Sterling and tries to have Spenser beaten up.

Ronan, Jeanette. (*Sudden Mischief*) The much younger, blonde wife of Francis Ronan; she has an affair with Brad Sterling.

Ronnie. (*Potshot*) Thug for Morris Tannenbaum who resembles an accountant.

Rosario, Paulie. (*Stone Cold*) One of the state police technicians working the scene at the Lincolns' apartment.

Rosen, Ike. (*Melancholy Baby*) Fat, disbarred attorney who hires thugs to beat up Sarah Markham.

Rosie. (*Family Honor, Perish Twice, Shrink Rap, Melancholy Baby*) Sunny Randall's miniature English bull terrier, fond of belly rubs and lapping faces.

Ross, Mrs. (*Ceremony*) Madam of a "sheep ranch" in Providence, RI, so called because it caters to some very special tastes; Spenser has to deal with her while searching for April Kyle.

Roth, Burton. (*Hush Money*) Ex-husband of stalking victim KC Roth.

Roth, KC, a.k.a. Katherine Carole. (*Hush Money*) A recently divorced friend of Susan, she needs help getting rid of a stalker, but she seems to want more from Spenser than he's willing to give.

Roth, Madelaine Reilly. (*Playmates*) Auburn-haired academic counselor for Taft University basketball player Dwayne Woodcock. She helps conceal Dwayne Woodcock's illiteracy and has ties to wiseguy Bobby Deegan and local hoodlum Gerry Broz.

Rowley, Marlene. (*Bad Business*) Suspecting that her husband, Trent Rowley, chief financial officer of Kinergy, is cheating on her, she asks Spenser to find the evidence.

Rowley, Trent. (*Bad Business*) Chief financial officer of the energy trading company Kinergy, he becomes the first murder victim in a case that gets increasingly complicated.

Royce, William, a.k.a. Hooker. (*Death in Paradise*) Star athlete and alleged boyfriend of murder victim Elinor Bishop.

Rudnick, Jean. (*Perchance to Dream*) Steely assistant of Randolph Simpson.

Rudy. (*Promised Land*) Informative bartender at the Silver Seas Motel in Hyannis.

Rugar. (*Small Vices, Cold Service*) Name used by the professional killer Spenser calls the Gray Man. In *Cold Service*, he is recommended by

Ives when Spenser needs a tough guy who speaks Ukrainian to infiltrate the Ukrainian mob in Marshport. He sometimes uses the pseudonym Kodi McKean.

St. Claire, Lisa. (*Thin Air*) The second wife of Frank Belson, she works as a disk jockey at a station in Proctor. When she goes missing, Spenser must help out his old friend and find her.

St. Claire, Madeleine. (*Thin Air, Night Passage*) Psychiatrist in Beverly Hills, who once treated Angela Richard. In *Night Passage* she is treating Jennifer Stone, Jesse Stone's ex-wife.

Salt, Tony. (*Trouble in Paradise*) News anchor at the station where Jennifer Stone is now working; he and Jennifer date for a while, and Jesse Stone isn't happy about it.

Salzman, Sandy. (*Stardust*) Line producer for the television show starring volatile actress Jill Joyce.

Sam. (*Shrink Rap*) Protective Akita of Kim Crawford.

Sampson, Craig. (*Walking Shadow*) Forty-one or forty-two-year-old actor in the Port City Theater Company; murder victim.

Samuelson, Lieutenant Mark. (*A Savage Place, Thin Air, Stardust, Potshot, Back Story*) Samuelson is the detective assigned to the murder of Mickey Rafferty in *A Savage Place*. Spenser later has him called in to arrest Peter Brewster for Candy Sloan's murder. In *Stardust* Spenser calls on him for information. In *Thin Air* once again he provides some information for Spenser, this time about Angela Richard. In *Potshot*, he has been promoted to captain, refers Mary Lou Buckman to Spenser, and provides Spenser with information on Steve Buckman. In *Back Story* he helps Spenser with information on a drug dealer named Coyote.

Sandborn, Marguerite. (*Family Honor*) Condescending therapist for Millicent Patton.

Sandy. (*Small Vices*) Attractive coed from Pemberton College whom Spenser chats up in a bar, digging for information on Melissa Henderson.

Santiago, Freddie. (*Thin Air*) Crime boss in Proctor, who would be very glad to see Luis Deleon out of the picture.

Santoro. (*Widow's Walk*) Norfolk County assistant district attorney involved in questioning Roy Levesque.

Sapp, Tedy. (*Hugger Mugger, Potshot*) Bodybuilding bouncer in the Bath House Bar and Grill, a gay bar, adept in karate; former deputy of Dalton Becker's and an army veteran. In *Potshot*, he joins Spenser's posse to rid Potshot, AZ, of the gang called the Dell.

Scanlan, Chuckie. (*Widow's Walk*) Associate of Jack DeRosa.

Schlossberg, a.k.a. Schlossie. (*Love and Glory*) Professor at Colby College who kicks Boone Adams out for sleeping in class.

Scott, Tiffany. (*Stardust*) Name of the girl reporter character that actress Jill Joyce played on an earlier television series.

Sears, Pat. (*Night Passage, Trouble in Paradise*) One of the patrol cops in the Paradise PD; he finds the corpse of Captain Cat. In *Trouble in Paradise* he is directing traffic near the scene of a suspected arson. He's killed in the line of duty later on in the book.

Sedale. (*Paper Doll*) An employee of the hotel where Spenser stays in Alton, SC. He leads Spenser to some key information.

Seltzer, Lennie. (*Mortal Stakes*, *Playmates*, *Chance*) Plump, pale-faced bookie who runs his business out of the Yorktown Tavern. Spenser seeks information from him on Marty Rabb. In *Playmates*, he provides Spenser with the results of Taft University basketball games. In *Chance*, he tells Spenser about Anthony Meeker's gambling habit.

Sewell, Joan. (*Double Play*) Wife of Walt Sewell.

Sewell, Walt. (*Double Play*) Reporter for *The Amsterdam News*.

Shaka. (*Back Story*) See Fancy, Abner.

Shark, The. (*Love and Glory*) Nickname for Guze's girlfriend.

Shaughnessy. (*All Our Yesterdays*) Boston beat cop who finds murder victim Maureen Burns.

Shaw, Norman. (*Death in Paradise*) Celebrated novelist who's giving a very lively party and isn't too happy when Jesse Stone wants him to quiet things down. He's acquainted with Gino Fish and plans to write a book about him.

Shaw, Joni. (*Death in Paradise*) Latest wife of novelist Norman Shaw.

Shawcross, Felton. (*Widow's Walk*) Fleshy CEO of Soldier's Field Development.

Shea, Kevin. (*Hugger Mugger*) Former boyfriend of Kate Malloy who is said to be stalking her; Spenser is hired to get rid of him.

Sheehan. (*Thin Air*) A cop in Proctor.

Shelley. (*Early Autumn*) One of the thugs employed by Harry Cotton.

Shepard, Harv. (*Promised Land*) A real estate developer who hires Spenser to find his runaway wife and is described by Spenser as Black Irish.

Shepard, Millie. (*Promised Land*) Pam and Harv Shepard's sixteen-year-old daughter.

Shepard, Pam. (*Promised Land*) Runaway wife who becomes involved in robbery and murder.

Sheridan, Augustus, a.k.a. Gus. (*All Our Yesterdays*) Son of Conn Sheridan, he is Boston's top homicide cop. He cares about only one thing, his son Chris, and will do anything to protect him, even destroy himself.

Sheridan, Chris. (*All Our Yesterdays*) The Harvard-educated son of Gus Sheridan and grandson of Conn Sheridan. His passionate love for Grace Winslow only complicates his family's tortured relationship with the Winslow clan.

Sheridan, Conn. (*All Our Yesterdays*) Patriarch of the Sheridan clan, former IRA fighter, and longtime Boston cop. Father of Gus and grandfather of Chris, he passes on to them a legacy of violence and corruption.

Sheridan, Mary Ellen Murphy, a.k.a. Mellen. (*All Our Yesterdays*) Devoutly Catholic wife of Conn Sheridan and mother of Gus.

Sheridan, Peggy Sheehan. (*All Our Yesterdays*) Alcoholic wife of Gus Sheridan and mother of Chris, who takes no interest in anyone but herself.

Shibell, Charlie. (*Gunman's Rhapsody*) Pima County, AZ, Sheriff, headquartered in Tucson.

Shoe. (*Double Deuce*) A member of the Hobart Street Raiders, he gets his hand caught in a van door by Spenser when Shoe attempts to shoot Hawk.

Shoney. (*Hugger Mugger*) Employee of Security South who fails to prevent Spenser's entry into the Clive house.

Shorty. (*Perchance to Dream*) A drunk with information on a Rancho Springs abandoned mineshaft.

Siegel, Marty. (*Bad Business*) An accountant Spenser calls in to perform an audit at Kinergy.

Silver, Daryl. (*Back Story*) Professional name used by Daryl Gordon. She seeks Spenser's help in finding out who murdered her mother during a bank robbery twenty-eight years before in Boston.

Silver, Mark. (*Bad Business*) Gay, attractive trainer who tells Spenser about Marlene Rowley's attempts to seduce him into an affair.

Silverman, Susan. A divorced guidance counselor at Smithfield's high school when she is introduced in *God Save the Child*. Spenser consults her during his investigation of Kevin Bartlett's disappearance, and they become involved with each other. In *Mortal Stakes* she comforts Spenser after his deadly showdown with Frank Doerr and Wally Hogg. In *Promised Land*, Susan and Spenser discuss their commitment to each other. In *The Judas Goat* she counsels Spenser on the psychology of one of the terrorists and eventually joins him in London for a post-case vacation. In *Looking for Rachel Wallace*, Susan accompanies Spenser to a dinner with Rachel Wallace. In *Early Autumn* she gives Spenser advice on dealing with the Giacomin family and, chiefly, with Paul. Spenser takes Paul to her cabin in Maine. In *Ceremony*, worried about one of her students, April Kyle, who has gone missing, she brings Spenser to talk to the girl's parents, one of whom doesn't want her back. In *The Widening Gyre*, Susan is interning in

Washington, D.C., and Spenser joins her there at the Hay Adams Hotel. In *Valediction* she graduates from Harvard with her Ph.D. and announces to Spenser that she is moving to San Francisco. In *A Catskill Eagle*, she calls on Hawk and Spenser for help in extricating her from her relationship with Russell Costigan. One of her clients is very likely the serial killer in *Crimson Joy*, and she must eventually decide whether to let Spenser confront the client with her. In *Double Deuce*, Susan and Spenser try living together. In *Walking Shadow*, Susan is a board member of a Boston-area theater company. In *Chance*, she accompanies Spenser to Las Vegas. In *Sudden Mischief*, Susan asks Spenser to investigate a sexual harassment complaint involving her ex-husband Brad Sterling. In *Hugger Mugger*, she accompanies Spenser to Saratoga to see Hugger Mugger win the Hopeful. In *Melancholy Baby*, she is Sunny Randall's therapist.

Simms, Rollie. (*A Savage Place*) Chief of security for Oceania Industries who shoots Candy Sloan.

Simpson, Harry. (*Poodle Springs*) Lawyer for Harlan Potter who springs Marlowe from jail.

Simpson, Herb. (*Hugger Mugger*) Employee of Security South who tails Spenser badly.

Simpson, Luther, a.k.a. Suitcase. (*Night Passage, Death in Paradise, Stone Cold*) Sharp young cop in the Paradise PD, nicknamed for a ball player. Jesse Stone very quickly sees his potential and comes to rely on him. In *Death in Paradise* he helps Jesse Stone stake out Gino Fish's office in Boston. In *Stone Cold* he finds the first victim of the serial killers.

Simpson, Nancy. (*Perish Twice*) Hal Reagan's girlfriend.

Simpson, Randolph. (*Perchance to Dream*) High-voiced, wealthy and warped, he has ties to the Resthaven sanitarium and California politicos.

Sippy, Ben. (*Gunman's Rhapsody*) City marshal after Fred White.

Sister Mary John. (*Family Honor, Death in Paradise*) A Catholic shelter worker who remembers seeing the missing Millicent Patton in *Family Honor*. In *Death in Paradise* Jesse Stone follows the trail of murder victim Elinor Bishop to Sister Mary John in Jamaica Plan, and the nun gives him some helpful information.

Slade, Deke. (*Promised Land*) Captain of the Barnstable, MA, Township Police Department.

Sloan, Candy. (*A Savage Place*) KNBS-TV reporter attempting to uncover a mob connection to the film industry; Spenser is hired by her station to protect her. In later books, Spenser is often haunted by feelings of failure over the outcome of this case.

Smith, Harry and Rocky. (*Trouble in Paradise*) The false names used by Macklin and Faye in Paradise.

Smith, Linda. (*Looking for Rachel Wallace*) Somewhat worshipful author escort for Rachel Wallace.

Smith, Mary Toricelli. (*Widow's Walk*) Dim wife of wealthy bank owner Nathan Smith who is accused of murdering him.

Smith, Nathan. (*Widow's Walk*) Financier and bank owner with a secret life; murder victim.

Smith, Willie. (*Love and Glory*) Black activist involved in voter registration efforts in Mississippi. Boone Adams and Jennifer Merchent listen to his speech at Taft University.

Snow, Pauline. (*Perchance to Dream*) Tough publisher of the *Rancho Springs Gazette and Chronicle*.

Snyder, Jerry. (*Death in Paradise*) Abusive husband who goes off the deep end when his wife finally leaves him.

Snyder, Vivian. (*Death in Paradise*) Battered wife of Jerry Snyder; she denies anything is wrong until finally she can't take any more.

Sonny. (*The Godwulf Manuscript*) Thug of crime boss Joe Broz. He unsuccessfully attempts to pound Spenser.

Sonny. ("Harlem Nocturne") Henchman of mob figure Frank Digiacomo.

Spellman, Sherry. (*Valediction*) Young dancer and girlfriend of Tommy Banks, she was once a member of the Reorganized Church of the Redemption. Abducted by them away from Banks, she claims she is happy to be with the church once again and away from the control of Tommy Banks.

Spike. (*Family Honor, Perish Twice, Shrink Rap, Melancholy Baby*) Actor and gay childhood friend of Sunny Randall; restaurant co-owner; karate expert and all-around tough guy. Sunny likens him to "a pleasant Kodiak bear" (*Shrink Rap* 136). In *Family Honor* and *Perish Twice*, he provides backup muscle to Sunny. In *Shrink Rap*, he relieves Sunny in bodyguard duties for Melanie Joan Hall. In *Melancholy Baby*, he beats up thugs threatening Sunny.

Stabile, Rick. (*Mortal Stakes*) Overweight Boston Red Sox pitcher whom Bucky Maynard criticizes on air.

Stanley (*Potshot*) Handsome young gay assistant of Gino Fish.

Stapleton, Clint. (*Small Vices*) Star tennis player at Taft College and former boyfriend of murdered coed Melissa Henderson.

Stapleton, Dina. (*Small Vices*) Adoptive mother of college tennis star Clint Stapleton.

Stapleton, Donald. (*Small Vices*) Wealthy and powerful, he doesn't take kindly to Spenser's questions about his adoptive son, Clint Stapleton.

Starzinski. (*Double Play*) A big Marine from Scranton, he is beaten up by Burke while they are serving in World War II.

Steele, Arnie. (*Poodle Springs*) Former California crime boss now settled in Poodle Springs.

Steiger. (*Wilderness*) Professional killer hired to get rid of Aaron Newman so he can't testify against Adolph Karl.

Stein, Barbara. (*Melancholy Baby*) Attorney for George, Barbara, and Sarah Markham who engages Sunny Randall to find Sarah Markham's birth parents.

Sterling, Brad, nee Silverman. (*Sudden Mischief*) Susan's tanned ex-husband turned charity fund raiser; fond of hitting family up for money and multiple infidelities.

Sternwood, Carmen. (*Perchance to Dream*) Severely disturbed daughter of General Sternwood and sister of Vivian Regan.

Sternwood, General Guy. (*Perchance to Dream*) Deceased father of Carmen Sternwood and Vivian Regan; hires Marlowe in Chandler's *The Big Sleep*.

Steven. (*Mortal Stakes*) Patricia Utley's butler-cum-bodyguard. He appears again in *Taming a Sea-Horse* and *Small Vices*.

Stone, Jennifer. (*Night Passage*, *Trouble in Paradise*, *Death in Paradise*, *Stone Cold*) Jesse Stone's ex-wife, with whom he has a troubled and emotionally tangled relationship. In *Trouble in Paradise* she has taken a job as a "weather girl" on a local television station. She assaults a woman who is unhappy with the way Jesse is handling a particular case and ends up in jail.

Stone, Jesse. (*Back Story*) Chief of police in Paradise; he gets inquisitive when he finds Spenser and Hawk on a stakeout on his turf. He is the main character in *Night Passage*, *Trouble in Paradise*, *Death in Paradise*, and *Stone Cold*.

Stratton, Bob. (*Paper Doll*) A senator who seems to know more about Olivia Nelson than he really should.

Suki. (*Taming a Sea-Horse*) Asian prostitute who offers her services to Spenser when he is investigating undercover at the Crown Prince Club in the Caribbean.

Sullivan, Liam. (*All Our Yesterdays*) An IRA man who assists in Conn Sheridan's escape from Kilmainham jail.

Sullivan, Michael. (*All Our Yesterdays*) Boston's police commissioner.

Summers, Ann. (*Paper Doll*) Secretary to Loudon Tripp, she is perhaps more loyal to her boss than he deserves.

Summers, Lilly, Dr. (*Death in Paradise*) Principal of Swampscott High School, where Jesse Stone goes in search of information on his unidentified murder victim. She and Jesse date briefly.

Swayze, Mrs. (*Perchance to Dream*) A vague old resident of Resthaven, she provides Marlowe with information about Carmen Sternwood.

Sylvia, Jackie. (*Promised Land*) New Bedford detective in charge of the bank robbery case in which Pam Shepard is involved.

Tabor, Mark. (*The Godwulf Manuscript*) Political counselor of SCACE (Student Committee Against Capitalist Exploitation). Spenser, who likens him to a zinnia, roughs him up to obtain information.

Taffy. (*Night Passage*) Girlfriend of Elliott Krueger, when Jesse Stone first meets Krueger.

Taggert, Clarice. (*Widow's Walk*) Black director of corporate giving at Illinois Federal Bank who provides details to Spenser on Mary Smith's fundraisers.

Tallboy. (*Double Deuce*) Boozy, sixteen-year-old member of the Dillard Street Posse gang; father of murder victim Crystal Jefferson; murder victim.

Tartabull, Vincent, a.k.a. Vinnie. (*Perchance to Dream*) Employee of the Rancho Springs Development Corporation and Gardenia-Tartabull Insurance and Real Estate.

Tatum, Ty-Bop. (*Sudden Mischief, Back Story, Cold Service, Family Honor, Perish Twice, Trouble in Paradise*) Skinny, twenty-year-old black shooter for local crime boss Tony Marcus. In *Back Story* he helps protect Spenser and Susan as a favor Marcus owes Hawk. In *Cold Service*, still working for Marcus, he's part of the operation to take out the Ukrainian mob. In *Family Honor*, he pulls a gun to protect Sunny Randall from Cathal Kragan. In *Perish Twice*, he serves as Marcus's bodyguard at a meeting with Desmond Burke. He makes a brief appearance with his boss in *Trouble in Paradise*.

Taylor, Abby. (*Night Passage, Trouble in Paradise, Stone Cold*) Lawyer with a local firm in Paradise, MA, who serves also as the town's legal counsel. She and Jesse have a brief relationship. In *Trouble in Paradise* she is dating other men and is retained by the Jencks family to represent Snapper. In *Stone Cold* she represents Bo Marino and comes to Jesse Stone's office with Bo's father, Joe. She is also a victim of the serial killers.

Taylor, Bebe. (*Potshot*) Lascivious wife of J. George Taylor, also in the real estate business, who makes a pass at Spenser.

Taylor, Dolores. (*Crimson Joy*) One of the victims of the Red Rose Killer.

Taylor, Eddie. (*Promised Land*) Egotistical weightlifter lover of Pam Shepard. Spenser decks him when he picks a fight with Spenser.

Taylor, J. George. (*Potshot*) Real estate agent in Potshot, AZ.

Taylor, John. (*The Widening Gyre*) A college student majoring in finance and campaign worker for Meade Alexander who is roughed up by the opposition, causing Spenser to step in.

Taylor, Nick. (*Love and Glory*) Tall boyfriend of Jennifer Grayle at Colby College who proposes to her and is rejected.

Teitler, Felicia Feinman Shaw. (*Death in Paradise*) Former wife of novelist Norman Shaw; she gives Jesse Stone some of the dirt on her former husband.

Teitler, Meredith. (*Hush Money*) Former employee at Hall, Peary, who was the victim of a stalker.

Temple, Lillian. (*Hush Money*) Professor in the English department who served on the committee that denied Robinson Nevins tenure.

Terry. (*Potshot*) Brunette girlfriend of Bernard J. Fortunato.

Thomas, Linda. (*Valediction*) For a long time she's just the girl who works in the office building across from Spenser's own office. With Susan gone, Spenser decides it's time to meet Linda. They hit it off, until the realities of Spenser's job begin to intrude.

Thompson, Dierdre. (*Walking Shadow*) Big-haired actress with the Port City Theater Company who calls Spenser "hunk city."

Thorson. (*Poodle Springs*) Indiscreet Poodle Springs realtor.

Ticknor, John. (*Looking for Rachel Wallace*) Executive with Hamilton Black Publishing, publisher of Rachel Wallace, who hires Spenser to protect Wallace.

Tillis, Orestes. (*Double Deuce*) Fat black minister who sounds like Paul Robeson and asks Hawk to remove the gangs from the Double Deuce housing project; calls Spenser "the white Satan."

Tillman. (*Hush Money*) Professor from the Law School who heads the university committee reconsidering the decision on Robinson Nevins's denial of tenure.

Timmons. (*Looking for Rachel Wallace*) Director of employee relations at First Mutual Insurance whom Spenser throws over the cafeteria serving counter.

Tinkham, Jimmy. (*Wilderness*) Young cop who, with Ed Diamond, responds to Aaron Newman's call about witnessing a murder.

Tino. (*Potshot*) Sharp-beaked thug who attempts to beat up Spenser in Santa Monica.

Toomy, Earl. (*Love and Glory*) Black supervisor of Boone Adams at Conray in Cleveland.

Tower, Carl. (*The Godwulf Manuscript*) Head of university security. He has Spenser thrown off campus when Spenser refuses to end his investigation into the Powell murder.

Trask, George. (*God Save the Child*) Overweight chief of the Smithfield Police; lover of Margery Bartlett.

Trenton, Reverend. (*Crimson Joy*) One of a group who confronts Martin Quirk with its concerns over the conduct of the investigation into the Red Rose killings.

Tripp, Dr. (*Hush Money*) On-call gynecologist at the hospital where Spenser takes KC Roth after she is assaulted.

Tripp, Loudon. (*Paper Doll*) Scion of a prominent New England family and a wealthy businessman, he hires Spenser to find out who brutally murdered his wife, Olivia Nelson, since the police seem unable to do so.

Tripp, Loudon, Jr., a.k.a. Chip. (*Paper Doll*) Twenty-two-year-old son of Loudon and Olivia Nelson.

Tripp, Meredith. (*Paper Doll*) Eighteen-year-old daughter of Loudon and Olivia Nelson.

Tripp, Olivia. See **Nelson, Olivia.**

Trish. (*Small Vices*) New girlfriend of Clint Stapleton.

Trumps. (*Ceremony*) Pimp in Boston's Combat Zone who tangles with Spenser and comes out the loser.

Tsyklins'kyj, Vanko. (*Cold Service*) Member of the Ukrainian mob and one of the men with whom Hawk has a score to settle.

Tuttle, Mr. (*Crimson Joy*) From the Christian United Action Committee; he is one of a group who comes to confront Martin Quirk over the investigation into the Red Rose killings.

Ty-Bop. See **Tatum, Ty-Bop.**

Tyler, Brinkman, a.k.a. Brink. (*Widow's Walk*) Broker for Nathan Smith; murder victim.

Tyler, John. (*Gunman's Rhapsody*) Big man who confronts Doc Holliday in the Oriental Saloon.

Utley, Patricia. (*Ceremony, Taming a Sea-Horse, Small Vices, Mortal Stakes*) High-class madam on the Midtown East Side in Manhattan who once employed Donna Burlington. She reappears in *Ceremony*, when Spenser asks for her help in finding a place for troubled teenager April Kyle. In *Taming a Sea-Horse* she asks Spenser to persuade April Kyle to come back to her job, after April has left to work for another call house. In *Small Vices* she aids Spenser in his search to make contact with the hit man Rugar.

Val. (*Poodle Springs*) Informative red-haired barfly at Reno's café.

Valdez, Eric. (*Pale Kings and Princes*) Reporter for the *Central Argus*; ladies' man; murder victim.

Valenti, Bob. (*Death in Paradise*) Part-time animal officer in Paradise, MA. In *Stone Cold* he finds a dog belonging to the first victim of the serial killers.

Valentine, Les, a.k.a. Larry Victor. (*Poodle Springs*) Photographer leading a double life.

Valentine, Muriel Blackstone, a.k.a. Muffy. (*Poodle Springs*) Daughter of Clayton Blackstone and wife of Les Valentine.

Vallone, Rudolph. (*Hugger Mugger*) Attorney with a Vandyke beard who represents the Clive estate and Dolly Hartman. He is described as having "about his person the faint aura of bay rum and good cigars and satisfying fees" (*Hugger Mugger* 163).

Vance, Marcy. (*Small Vices*) Once a young public defender, she now works in a prestigious firm with Rita Fiore. They ask Spenser to investigate one of Marcy's old cases to determine whether the right man is in jail for murder.

Vargas, Sergeant. (*Stone Cold*) State police sergeant who talks with Jesse Stone, offering assistance from the state cops to deal with the serial killings.

Velvet, a.k.a. Kim Pak Soong. (*Sudden Mischief*) A Korean prostitute working for local crime boss Tony Marcus, she arranges with Spenser for him to be present at her next rendezvous with Haskell Wechsler.

Ventura, Iris. (*Chance*) Wife of Boston crime boss Julius Ventura.

Ventura, Julius. (*Chance*) Boston crime boss who hires Spenser to find his missing son-in-law.

Vern. (*Perchance to Dream*) Fat, abusive sergeant in Rancho Springs, CA.

Vic. (*Chance*) The efficient bouncer at the topless Starlight Lounge.

Vicki. (*Potshot*) Receptionist for movie producer Mark Ratliff.

Victor, Angel. (*Poodle Springs*) Larry Victor's trusting wife.

Victor, Larry. See **Valentine, Les.**

Vigilant Virgin. (*Pastime*) Registered name of Pearl, the solid chocolate German shorthair pointer that becomes the canine companion of Spenser and Susan from this book on.

Vincent, Duke. (*Night Passage, Stone Cold*) Young EMT worker who hasn't seen much violent death. In *Stone Cold* he gets further exposure to victims of violent death.

Vincent, Louis. (*Hush Money*) Stockbroker boyfriend of KC Roth who, despite the fact that he has ended their relationship, could be KC's stalker.

Vincent, Murray, Lieutenant. (*Wilderness*) State policeman who, along with Bobby Croft, is very interested in Aaron Newman's testimony about the murder he witnessed.

Violet. (*Mortal Stakes*) New York City pimp for whom Donna Burlington once worked.

Virgie. (*Pale Kings and Princes*) Close-mouthed female bartender at the restaurant of the Reservoir Court, Spenser's motel in Wheaton.

Vogel, Dr. (*The Godwulf Manuscript*) Chair of the university English department.

Vollmer, Ray. (*Night Passage*) Deputy in the Campbell County, WY, Sheriff's Department who is on the scene of Tom Carson's accident.

Vong. (*Trouble in Paradise*) Associate of Bo Chang, who's doing a drug deal with Crow, one of Macklin's gang.

Voss, Sergeant. (*Trouble in Paradise*) Security man at a poker game where Macklin makes off with all the money. Macklin shoots him before he leaves.

Vowel, Orotund. (*Crimson Joy*) The name Spenser gives when he is confronted by a group of irate citizens in Martin Quirk's office; he claims to be Quirk's elocution teacher.

Wagner, Harold. (*Playmates*) Black history professor at Taft University who suspected that Dwayne Woodcock was illiterate.

Wally. (*Pale Kings and Princes*) Proprietor of Wally's Lunch in Wheaton; Spenser likens him to "a toad" (*Pale Kings and Princes* 57).

Walker, Dean. (*Potshot*) Chief of police in Potshot, AZ; formerly a cop in Santa Monica, CA.

Walker, Dixie. (*Chance*) Topless waitress at the Starlight Lounge and former girlfriend of Anthony Meeker.

Walker, Judy. (*Potshot*) Ex-wife of Dean Walker.

Wallace, Judge. (*Gunman's Rhapsody*) Judge who hears a case against Ike Clanton.

Wallace, Rachel. (*Looking for Rachel Wallace, A Catskill Eagle, Sudden Mischief*) Lesbian author of *Sisterhood* and *Tyranny*; in *Looking for Rachel Wallace* Spenser is engaged by her publisher as her bodyguard. In *A Catskill Eagle*, she provides information on Jerry Costigan to Spenser. In *Sudden Mischief*, she is in Boston for a lecture and provides some insight to Spenser on Susan and Brad Sterling.

Walsh, Melanie. (*The Widening Gyre*) Campaign worker for Meade Alexander who is roughed up by the opposition, causing Spenser to step in.

Walter, Bruce. (*Love and Glory*) Classmate of Boone Adams at Colby College. He makes a pass at Jennifer Grayle.

Walters, Robert, a.k.a. Walt. (*Hush Money*) Friend and roommate of Prentice Lamont and co-conspirator in the work of outing prominent closeted figures.

Warren. (*A Catskill Eagle*) Fat security guard with skinny arms; also known as "The Counterman," as Hawk and Spenser first meet him in a store owned by Costigan.

Washburn, Emmeline. (*Crimson Joy*) One of the victims of the Red Rose Killer; or is she?

Washburn, Raymond. (*Crimson Joy*) Estranged husband of Emmeline, who has been murdered, allegedly by the Red Rose Killer.

Washington, Roy. (*Love and Glory*) Black former boxer who works for carpenter Henry Reagan with Boone Adams.

Wasserman, Phyllis. (*Hush Money*) Director of human resources at Hall, Peary, the firm where Louis Vincent works.

Waters, Walt. (*Love and Glory*) Boss of Boone Adams at the Discretionary Mutual Insurance Company of America.

Wax, Jacky. (*Taming a Sea-Horse*) Works for underworld figure Mr. Milo, who is protecting Perry Lehman.

Weatherwax, John. (*Taming a Sea-Horse*) See **Wax, Jacky.**

Wechsler, Haskell. (*Sudden Mischief*) Thick-lipped, fat, merciless loan-shark doing business with Brad Sterling and Richard Gavin, described by Spenser as "the worst man alive" (*Sudden Mischief* 199).

Wells, Julie. (*Looking for Rachel Wallace*) Model and lover of author Rachel Wallace.

West, Holly. (*Mortal Stakes*) Catcher for the Red Sox, well known for a Brut commercial, about which the other players tease him.

Westin, Abel. (*The Widening Gyre*) Media consultant for Congressman Meade Alexander.

White, Fred. (*Gunman's Rhapsody*) City marshal in Tombstone; killed in the line of duty.

Whitestone, Sergeant. (*Poodle Springs*) Cop from the Poodle Springs police department.

Whitfield, Warren. (*Taming a Sea-Horse*) Bank president with a penchant for prostitutes who is connected to the murder of Ginger Buckey and the disappearance of April Kyle.

Wilde, Taggert. (*Perchance to Dream*) A plump L.A. district attorney; former employer of Marlowe.

Willie. (*Poodle Springs*) Bartender at Reno's café in Los Angeles.

Willie, a.k.a. Fat Willie. (*Valediction*) Head of a crew of hit men who go after Spenser. Fat Willie and his crew don't fare too well.

Wilson, Doc. (*Mortal Stakes*) Former major league baseball player, he now does color commentary for the Boston Red Sox.

Winslow, Bonnie. (*Perish Twice*) Sometime girlfriend of Lawrence B. Reeves.

Winslow, Cabot. (*All Our Yesterdays*) Ineffectual son of Thomas Jr. and Laura Winslow; brother of Grace Winslow. His father's intention to buy Cabot a Senate seat leads to a final face-off between the Sheridans and the Winslows.

Winslow, Grace. (*All Our Yesterdays*) Daughter of Thomas Winslow, Jr. In love with Chris Sheridan, she is wary of the rage and all-consuming passion he seems to have for her.

Winslow, Hadley, Mrs. (*All Our Yesterdays*) Wife of prominent Bostonian Thomas Winslow, Sr., and passionate lover of Conn Sheridan. Her betrayal of him will have far-reaching consequences.

Winslow, Laura. (*All Our Yesterdays*) The wife of Thomas Winslow, Jr., she is inured to a passionless marriage, but is completely unaware of her husband's true nature. Mother of Grace and Cabot Winslow.

Winslow, Thomas, Sr. (*All Our Yesterdays*) Prominent, wealthy Bostonian, husband of Hadley, father of Thomas Jr., who has little idea of his wife's infidelities or his son's acts of perversion.

Winslow, Thomas, Jr. (*All Our Yesterdays*) Son of Hadley and Thomas Sr. and father of Grace Winslow. His perversions give the Sheridans a hold over his family for a long time.

Winston, Bullard. (*Valediction*) Head of the religious organization the Reorganized Church of the Redemption, whose members are often called "Bullies." Spenser tangles with him several times in his efforts to free Sherry Spellman from the Bullies.

Winston, Jimmy. (*Crimson Joy*) Host of a popular call-in radio show; he invites Spenser on to talk about the Red Rose Killer.

Witherspoon, Race. (*God Save the Child*, *Widow's Walk*) Gay fashion photographer. In *God Save the Child*, he provides Spenser with information on Vic Harroway. In *Widow's Walk*, he tells Spenser about Nathan Smith's secret life.

Woodcock, Dwayne. (*Playmates*) Six-foot-nine, black power forward for the Taft University basketball team who cannot read; he likes to refer to himself in the third person. He is suspected of point shaving.

Worthy, Dr. (*Shrink Rap*) Gynecologist of Sally Millwood.

Wu, Lonnie (*Walking Shadow*) Owner of a Chinese restaurant called Wu's in Port City; husband of Port City Theater Company board member Rikki Wu. Smuggler of illegal Chinese immigrants who has ties to organized crime; murder victim.

Wu, Rikki. (*Walking Shadow*) Board member of the Port City Theater Company; spoiled wife of restaurant owner Ronnie Wu; sister of local Chinese organized crime boss Eddie Lee.

Wyatt, Cord. (*Hugger Mugger*) Husband of Stonie Wyatt and closeted gay man with a preference for boys.

Wyatt, Stonie. (*Hugger Mugger*) Daughter of Walter Clive who worked as a prostitute for kicks.

Wyman, Patti. (*Love and Glory*) Librarian and lover of Boone Adams in Los Angeles.

Yan. (*Walking Shadow*) Seventeen-year-old member of the Asian street gang the Death Dragons. He tries to kill Spenser twice.

Yates, Captain. (*The Godwulf Manuscript*) Martin Quirk's superior who takes Quirk off the Powell case in response to pressure from above.

Zabriskie, Jillian. (*Stardust*) Real name of television star Jill Joyce.

Zabriskie, Vera. (*Stardust*) Mother of actress Jill Joyce.

Zabriskie, William, a.k.a. Bill. (*Stardust*) Estranged father of television star Jill Joyce.

Zachary. (*The Judas Goat*) Former weightlifter turned terrorist who is an associate of Paul, the head of the group Liberty.

Zeecond, Melvin, a.k.a. Zeke. (*A Savage Place*) Hollywood agent and former lover of Candy Sloan who has the goods on Summit Studios.

A ROBERT B. PARKER GAZETTEER

The city of Boston features prominently in all of the Spenser novels and in some of the nonseries works as well, chiefly in *All Our Yesterdays*. Spenser's work is not confined to Boston, however, and over the course of the series, he travels quite a bit. Not just around the Boston area, but around the country and even to Europe. The Jesse Stone books are set in the fictional town of Paradise, Massachusetts, but Sunny Randall's Boston is the same as Spenser's, and there is some overlap of characters and places among the three series. We have endeavored to catalog as many places in the books as possible, at least where major action takes place. We have not listed every bar where a character drops in for a drink, nor every restaurant where a character has a meal, however.

In a way, Boston is as important a character in the Spenser novels as Spenser himself, or Hawk or Susan Silverman. The city, in all its many guises, with its rich history, provides a fascinating backdrop for crime novels, and Parker makes superb use of the city time and time again.

Alton, SC. In *Paper Doll* Spenser spends quite a bit of time here, seeking background information on the murdered Olivia Nelson. In *Hug-*

ger Mugger, a horse that may relate to Spenser's case in Lamarr, GA, is shot here.

Amsterdam, the Netherlands. In *The Judas Goat* Spenser and Hawk track their quarry here, after Copenhagen. They stay at the Marriott.

Andover, MA. Where Mel Giacomin lives, and where he's keeping his son Paul, in *Early Autumn*. In *Small Vices* Spenser visits Hunt and Glenda McMartin at their home here, to talk about the Melissa Henderson case. It's also the location of Barbara Stein's law office and the Markhams' residence in *Melancholy Baby*.

The Aquarium (Boston). Spenser goes here to cool off and think about his visit with Bucky Maynard at Harbor Towers in *Mortal Stakes*.

Arlington, MA. Where Spenser goes, in *Small Vices*, to confront Bruce Parisi about his connection to the Melissa Henderson case. In *Bad Business* private eye Elmer O'Neill has his office here, in a converted gas station. In *Shrink Rap*, Kerry Crawford's real estate office is located here.

Assembly Square (Boston). Spenser takes Linda Thomas here to see a movie, and things quickly get complicated afterwards, in *Valediction*.

Back Bay (Boston). The area in Boston where Mitchell Poitras lives in *Ceremony*. In *Paper Doll* Spenser meets Loudon Tripp for lunch at the Harvard Club. Brad Sterling has an office here in *Sudden Mischief*. In *Perish Twice*, Natalie Goddard has an apartment here and eats lunch at the Ritz with Mary Lou Goddard. In *Double Play*, Joseph Burke meets his future wife Carole here at a USO dance.

Bay Tower Room (Boston). Spenser goes on a double date with Hawk to this exclusive restaurant with a great view of Boston Harbor in *Valediction*.

Bay Village. Location of the gay bar Nellie's in *Widow's Walk*.

Beacon Hill (Boston). The exclusive area of Boston where the Tripp family lives on Louisburg Square, in *Paper Doll*. Spenser visits the Tripp home, seeking information on the murdered Olivia Nelson. In *All Our Yesterdays* the Winslows live here.

Bedford, MA. Location of the home of Brad Sterling's sister in *Sudden Mischief*.

Beecham, ME. Where Last Stand Systems is located, in *Hush Money*.

Bel Air, CA. In *Stardust*, Spenser goes to the home of Victor del Rio, seeking information on Jill Joyce's past. Home of the wealthy Clayton Blackstone in *Poodle Springs*.

Belfast, ME. Town on Penobscot Bay on the Maine coast where Brett Rogers picks up, and Spenser follows, a cocaine shipment in *Pale Kings and Princes*.

Berkeley Street (Boston). Location of Spenser's office, two blocks from police headquarters.

Beverly, MA. In *Pastime* Spenser and Hawk have a meeting with Gerry Broz at a restaurant called Rocco's Grotto on Rantoul Street. In *Bad Business* Spenser talks with lawyer Randy Frampton at the offices of Frampton and Keyes here.

Beverly Farms, MA. In *All Our Yesterdays* the Winslows have a house here, and they host a party for Chris Sheridan.

Boise, ID. Location of a silver mine converted by Jerry Costigan in *A Catskill Eagle*, where Spenser tracks him down.

Boston, MA. Spenser has a picnic with Brenda Loring in the Public Garden in *Mortal Stakes*. In *Early Autumn* Spenser and Susan Silverman go to a Celtics game in the Garden. In *Valediction* Spenser searches for information on Bullard Winston and his church at the Kirstein Business Library off School Street. He follows this up with a visit to the State House, looking for more information. During the filming of the show *Fifty Minutes*, some of the crew's trailers are situated on the Common, in *Stardust*. The production office for the show is on Soldiers Field Road. Jill Joyce, the television star, is staying in the Charles Hotel. Near the end of *Pastime* Spenser has a confrontation with Gerry Broz in the Public Gardens. In *Back Story*, Spenser visits the Boston FBI office in One Center Plaza and later consults with the "International Consulting Bureau" in the New Federal Courthouse on Fan Pier. The city is also home to the Sheridan and Winslow clans, in *All Our Yesterdays*.

Boston College. Spenser chats with a priest there in *Valediction* to find out more about a religious group.

Boston Public Library. In *Looking for Rachel Wallace*, Spenser goes to the Boston Public Library to research the Belmont Vigilance Committee. In *Sudden Mischief*, he goes there to read back issues of the *Boston Globe* to learn about Galapalooza.

Bow Lake, MA. The site of Evan Malone's cabin, in *Back Story*.

Boxford, MA. Location of Ann Riley's house in *Widow's Walk*; a "big honky development," according to Hawk (*Widow's Walk* 154).

Boylston Street (Boston). In *Early Autumn*, Spenser has moved his office to the second floor of a building on the corner of Boylston and Berkeley Streets.

Brant Island. A birdwatchers' venue that is north of Port City. In *Walking Shadow*, Spenser hides there and sees illegal immigrants from China coming ashore.

Braves Field (Boston). Where Conn Sheridan takes Mellen Murphy on a Saturday outing, in *All Our Yesterdays*.

Breakhart Reservation, Saugus, MA. Where Spenser sets up a showdown with the bad guys in *Mortal Stakes*.

Brighton, MA. Suburb of Boston. In *Playmates*, Spenser and Hawk go to the B&D coffee shop in Brighton to talk to Joe Broz's son Gerry (whom Spenser investigated in *The Widening Gyre*). In *Sudden Mischief*, Brighton is the location of the apartment of the cash-strapped Brad Sterling. In *Perish Twice*, Sunny Randall's friend Julie has an abortion at a Brighton clinic. In *Melancholy Baby*, Randall meets attorney Lewis Karp at a Brighton coffee shop.

Brookline, MA. Where murder victim Melissa Henderson's parents live, in *Small Vices*.

Brooklyn, NY. The Dodgers play at Ebbets Field in *Double Play*.

Brunswick, ME. In *Thin Air*, where Spenser tracks down Lisa St. Claire's father.

Buckhead, GA. Upwardly mobile suburb north of Atlanta where Jon Delroy's Security South has an office in *Hugger Mugger*. Spenser and Susan stay in a Ritz-Carlton hotel in Buckhead in *Potshot*.

Buddy's Fox (Boston). A restaurant in the South End of Boston, which serves as Tony Marcus's headquarters. Spenser and Hawk go to see Marcus in *Ceremony*. In *Cold Service* it has been renamed "Ebony & Ivory."

Burlington, VT. Sunny Randall accompanies Melanie Joan Hall on a book tour to the Barnes & Noble here in *Shrink Rap*.

Café Vendome (Boston). Place in Boston on Commonwealth Avenue where Spenser stops for a meal in *Ceremony*.

Cambridge, MA. Where Susan Silverman lives, one hundred yards up from the common, and later on Linnaean Street. Also home to Harvard University. In *Playmates*, Spenser and Susan have dinner at the Rarities restaurant in the Charles Hotel in Cambridge. In *Double Deuce*, Susan's house is located on Linnaean Street and doubles as her office. In *Sudden Mischief*, Spenser and Hawk have a drink and some pan-fried oysters at the bar in the Casablanca in Harvard Square. Sunny Randall and Julie also go to the bar at the Casablanca twice in *Perish Twice*, which also is a pickup place for Lawrence B. Reeves. In *Sudden Mischief*, Spenser and Susan go for a run on the Cambridge side of the Charles River, near the Cambridge Boat Club. In *Widow's Walk*, Spenser, Susan, Hawk, and Estelle Raphael have dinner in the Hyatt Hotel in Cambridge, and Spenser talks to Marvin Conroy in the Cambridge Galleria. In *Family Honor*, Sunny Randall and Julie have tea in LouLou's in Harvard Square. In *Perish Twice*, Sunny Randall goes to Cambridge to confront Lawrence B. Reeves, and her friend Julie moves here when she leaves her husband. In *Shrink Rap*, Randall and Julie have dinner at the Cambridge restaurant Cuchi Cuchi, and Randall and author Melanie Joan Hall eat lunch at Full Moon. In *Love and Glory*, Boone Adams works part time for a carpentry contractor in Cambridge, and he and Jennifer Merchent go to a graduate student party there. In *All Our Yesterdays* Chris Sheridan has a half-house condo here.

Canton, MA. In *Bad Business* Spenser and Hawk take Hawk's girlfriend Cecile here, so she can do some undercover work at the Balmoral Castle Hotel.

Cape Cod, MA. Setting (and analogy) for *Promised Land*. "Living around Boston a long time you tend to think of Cape Cod as the promised land. Sea, sun, sky, health, ease, boisterous camaraderie, a kind of real-life beer commercial." (*Promised Land* 71–72).

Capitol Hill (Washington, D.C.). Spenser noses around Capitol Hill in Washington, D.C., for information on Gerry Broz and is hauled there to confront Congressman Robert Browne in *The Widening Gyre*.

Charles River (Boston). Spenser often runs along the river when he's exercising.

Charles River Dam. In *Valediction* Spenser faces off with several hired killers here.

Charles River Park. Site of Brenda Loring's apartment in Boston in *Mortal Stakes*.

Charlestown, MA. Site of Frank Doerr's funeral parlor, where Spenser goes to have a talk with Doerr in *Mortal Stakes*. When the CIA find a safe house for Spenser and Hawk in *A Catskill Eagle*, Spenser and Hawk ridicule the CIA agents for their lack of sense, because Hawk does not blend in with the surroundings in this white-bread neighborhood of Boston.

Chelsea, MA. In *Promised Land*, Spenser meets with loan shark King Powers at the market terminal in Chelsea, which is described by Spenser as "a shabby town, beloved by its residents, across the Mystic River in Boston" (192). It is the site of the sting operation involving a pair of radical feminists and Powers.

Chestnut Hill, MA. Where Mel Giacomin's girlfriend lives, in *Early Autumn*. It's also the location of Mary Lou Goddard's condo in *Perish Twice* and John Melvin's psychiatric practice in *Shrink Rap*.

Chicago, IL. Tyler Smithson Costigan's penthouse apartment is located on Lake Shore Drive in *A Catskill Eagle*. In *Love and Glory*, Boone Adams gets a job in a Coca-Cola bottling plant in Chicago. In *Double Play*, the Dodgers play the Cubs in Chicago, and Jackie Robinson is tagged in the face while sliding into second.

Chinatown (Boston). Conn Sheridan and Knocko Kiernan confront members of a Chinese tong over a murder here in *All Our Yesterdays*.

Church Park (Boston). A large, gray, cement urban development associated with the Christian Science church complex across the street on Massachusetts Avenue, where Marty and Linda Rabb live in *Mortal Stakes*.

Cincinnati, OH. Sunny Randall accompanies Melanie Joan Hall on a book tour to the Cincinnati suburbs in *Shrink Rap*. In *Double Play*, the Dodgers play the Reds there, and during the game Jackie Robinson is knocked down three times by the pitcher.

Cleveland, OH. Sunny Randall accompanies Melanie Joan Hall on a book tour here in *Shrink Rap*. They have a drink in the bar of the Stouffer's Tower Plaza on Public Square. In *Love and Glory*, Boone Adams gets a job at a company called Conray in Cleveland.

Combat Zone (Boston). The notorious area in Boston where prostitution and crime are rampant. Spenser searches through it to find April Kyle in *Ceremony*.

1010 Commonwealth Avenue (Boston). State police headquarters, where Spenser goes to talk to Healy in *Mortal Stakes*. Throughout the series there are occasional scenes here. In *Wilderness* Aaron Newman talks with state policemen Vincent and Croft here a couple of times.

Concord, MA. Spenser and Paul Giacomin travel here to talk to a close friend of Patty Giacomin, in *Pastime*. In *Walking Shadow*, Spenser and Susan buy a three-hundred-year-old farmhouse together in Concord to renovate and use as a weekend getaway. In *All Our Yesterdays* Gus Sheridan buys a house here, which he starts renovating after confessing everything to his son, Chris.

Copenhagen, Denmark. Spenser and Hawk follow their quarry here in *The Judas Goat*. They stay at the Sheraton and manage a bit of sightseeing at the famous Tivoli Gardens.

Copley Square (Boston). In the historic district of downtown Boston, Copley Square is the location of the Boston Public Library, Trinity Church, and the Copley Plaza Hotel. In *The Godwulf Manuscript*, Spenser has a deadly fight in the Copley Plaza, where Lowell Hayden is hiding out. In *Shrink Rap*, author Melanie Joan Hall has an apartment there.

Dallas, TX. In *Love and Glory*, Boone Adams works here as a dishwasher.

Danvers, MA. Spenser meets Sherry Spellman at the Liberty Tree Mall here in *Valediction*.

Dodge City, KS. Home to the Earp clan before most of them move to Tombstone, AZ.

Dover, MA. Where Stanley Rojack lives, in *Stardust*.

Dublin, Ireland. In *All Our Yesterdays*, where Conn Sheridan recuperates from his wounds, meets Hadley Winslow, and assassinates John Cooper. Chris Sheridan also tells Grace Winslow of his trip to Dublin, and its impact on him.

East Cambridge, MA. Location of the home branch of Pequod Savings & Loan in *Widow's Walk*.

Essex, MA. Marshy town north of Boston where Spenser and Susan eat fried clams and onion rings in *Sudden Mischief*.

Everett, MA. The site of Marty Martinelli's business, in *Pastime*. Rich Beaumont has a condo in a building on Revere Beach Boulevard.

Fair Harbor, CA. Near Redondo Beach, Fair Harbor is the site of the showdown between Marlowe and Randolph Simpson in *Perchance to Dream*.

The Fenway (Boston). The Fenway is an expanse of open green space near the Charles River and the location of Fenway Park where the Boston Red Sox play. It is the site of the showdown for Hawk, Spenser, and the Hobart Street Raiders in *Double Deuce*.

Fenway Park (Boston). An important setting for Spenser's investigation of Red Sox pitcher Marty Rabb in *Mortal Stakes*. In *All Our Yesterdays* Gus Sheridan takes his son Chris here.

The Fish Pier (Boston). Seedy section of the wharf of Boston Harbor. In *A Catskill Eagle*, Spenser and Hawk go to the Fish Pier to confront Jerry Costigan's men.

Fitchburg, MA. About fifty miles west of Boston and home to Fitchburg State College, where Spenser goes to attend a lecture by Milo Quant of Last Stand Systems, in *Hush Money*. It's also the home district of Congressman Meade Alexander in *The Widening Gyre*.

Fort Dix, NJ. Boone Adams is sent here after being drafted in *Love and Glory*.

Framingham, MA. Location of the office of plumber Kevin Humphries in *Family Honor*.

Franklin, MA. Location of Franklin High School in *Widow's Walk*.

Fryeburg, ME. Susan Silverman owns property near here, and Spenser takes Paul Giacomin here to help him build a cabin, in *Early Autumn*. In *Stardust* Spenser brings Jill Joyce to the cabin, hoping to give her some time to recuperate. In *Wilderness*, Aaron and Janet Newman, along with their friend Chris Hood, stalk Adolph Karl and his associates in the nearby woods.

Georgetown (Washington, D.C.). Well-to-do neighborhood in northwest Washington, D.C.; home of Congressman Meade Alexander and Georgetown University student Gerry Broz in *The Widening Gyre*.

Gloucester, MA. Where retired cop Mario Bennati lives, in *Back Story*.

Groveland, MA. Location of Sally Millwood's house in *Shrink Rap*. According to Sunny Randall, the town is "fifteen miles from nowhere" (*Shrink Rap* 184).

Harbor Health Club (Boston). Run by Henry Cimoli, it's the place where Spenser works out. Hawk also frequents it, and it's through the club and Henry that Spenser often can get in touch with Hawk when necessary.

Harbor Towers (Boston). New complex of high-rise apartments that looks out over Boston Bay; this is where Bucky Maynard lives in *Mortal Stakes*.

Harlem, New York City. In *Double Play,* Joseph Burke and Jackie Robinson have a confrontation with gangster Johnny Paglia in Paglia's

Harlem restaurant, and Burke consults with black racketeer Wendell Jackson there. In the story "Harlem Nocturne," the confrontation takes place with Robinson, the unnamed narrator, and gangster Frank Boucicault. Also in *Double Play*, Burke and Lauren Roach go to the Harlem nightclub The Plantation.

Harvard University (Cambridge, MA). In *Hush Money* Spenser and Hawk call on Amir Abdullah at the African-American Center. Other scenes in the book involve other locations around campus, while Spenser is working on Robinson Nevins's case. In *Back Story* Spenser and Hawk go for a run at the Harvard Stadium. Later on in the book, Spenser has a deadly confrontation at the stadium. In *All Our Yesterdays* Chris Sheridan is a student here, and later a professor of criminology.

Harvard Yard (Cambridge, MA). Spenser attends Susan Silverman's graduation at the opening of *Valediction*. Henceforth she is Dr. Silverman.

Haverhill, MA. In *Thin Air*, where Spenser goes looking for Lisa St. Claire's parents. It's the location of Mary Murphy Hospital in *Shrink Rap*.

Hollyford, Ireland. Village in mid-Tipperary where Conn Sheridan and fellow IRA members assault a barracks, in *All Our Yesterdays*.

Holy Cross Cathedral (Boston). The funeral mass for Conn Sheridan is held here in *All Our Yesterdays*.

Hyannis (Cape Cod, MA). Location of Harv Shepard's house in *Promised Land*.

International Place (Boston). A forty-story building across the street from Rowe's Wharf on the waterfront. In *Double Deuce*, Hawk and Spenser meet Tony Marcus here in a croissant shop.

Jamaica Plain, MA. Where the opening scene of *Crimson Joy* takes place. Belson takes Spenser here to see the scene of a what could be the latest in a string of serial murders. In *Thin Air*, Frank Belson and his wife, Lisa St. Claire, have an apartment here, near Brookline. In *Family Honor*, it's the location of the Catholic-run shelter where Millicent Patton sleeps.

Kenmore Square (Boston). Where Sunny Randall goes looking for the missing Millicent Patton after Red Sox games in *Family Honor*. In *Double Play*, the Brooklyn Dodgers stay at the Hotel Kenmore when they are in town to play the Braves.

Kennebunkport, ME. Where Spenser goes to talk to Sybil Pritchard in *Back Story*. In *Bad Business* Spenser and Susan Silverman have a picnic on a stone pier at the beach here.

Kilhainham Gaol (Dublin, Ireland). Where Conn Sheridan is imprisoned until his escape, in *All Our Yesterdays*.

King's Beach (Swampscott, MA). In *Crimson Joy* Spenser chases the killer on the beach.

Korea. Boone Adams is drafted and sent here in *Love and Glory*.

Lafayette Park (Washington, D.C.). Park adjacent to the White House and location of the Hay Adams Hotel, where Spenser stays when he visits Washington, D.C., in *The Widening Gyre*.

La Jolla, CA. Spenser and Hawk stay here, at La Valencia, while tracking down information on the Emily Gordon case, in *Back Story*.

Lamarr, GA. Location of Three Fillies Stables in *Hugger Mugger*. Spenser returns here in *Potshot* to recruit Tedy Sapp into his posse.

The Last Hurrah (Boston). The restaurant in which Spenser dines with Susan Silverman at the close of the Marty Rabb case in *Mortal Stakes*.

Las Vegas, NV. Hawk and Spenser travel to Las Vegas to track compulsive gambler Anthony Meeker in *Chance*. Spenser returns in *Potshot* to recruit detective Bernard J. Fortunato into his posse.

Lenox, MA. About two hours west of Boston on the Massachusetts Turnpike; Spenser and Paul Giacomin travel here, looking for Paul's missing mother, Patty Giacomin, in *Pastime*.

Lewis Wharf (Boston). Where Linda Thomas has a condo, in *Valediction*.

Lexington, MA. Patty Giacomin lives here, with her son Paul, in *Early Autumn*. In *Pastime* Paul and Spenser go once again to Patty's house, seeking information after Patty has seemingly disappeared.

Lincoln, MA. Where Bob and Wilma Cooper live, in *Bad Business*.

Lindell, ME. Where Spenser goes to confront Vern Buckey, in *Taming a Sea-Horse*.

Litchfield, CT. Location of the home of gangster Frank Boucicault and his son Louis in *Double Play*.

London, England. Spenser heads for London to track down the group responsible for the deaths of Hugh Dixon's family in *The Judas Goat*. While there he stays at the Hotel Mayfair near Berkeley Square. He dines at Simpson's with his police contacts. He manages to work in some sightseeing while he waits, taking in the National Gallery, the Tower of London, and the British Museum, among other famous sights. He sets up a meeting in Regent's Park near the London Zoo with one of the group responsible for the deaths of the Dixon family. After the conclusion of the case, Spenser goes back to London with Susan Silverman.

Long Beach, CA. Site of the Coast Guard station where Marlowe finds himself after his confrontation with Randolph Simpson in *Perchance to Dream*.

Los Angeles, CA. Spenser travels to L.A. to protect TV reporter Candy Sloan in *A Savage Place*. He describes it as "a big, sunny buffoon of a city; corny and ornate and disorganized but kind of fun . . . It was where we'd run out of room, where the dream had run up against the ocean, and human voices woke us" (*A Savage Place* 144). In *Stardust*, Spenser goes to Century City to talk to Jill Joyce's agent. He seeks out Jill's father, William Zabriskie, at his apartment in Hollywood. He also makes a visit to Candy Sloan's grave in Forest Lawn Cemetery. In *Thin Air* Spenser and Susan Silverman head west, looking for information on the background of Lisa St. Claire. He returns to Los Angeles in *Potshot* to consult with Captain Mark Samuelson and Vincent del Rio. In *Back Story* Spenser and Hawk spend time here, tracking down leads in the Emily Gordon case. In *Shrink Rap*, Sunny Randall accompanies author Melanie Joan Hall to Hollywood discuss a film deal of Hall's books and stays at the Beverly Wilshire Hotel. In *Poodle Springs*, Philip Marlowe looks for a missing photographer in L.A. and describes Hollywood as a place where "movie stars, directors, producers, agents, people . . . had found a way to package emptiness and sell it as dreams" (*Poodle Springs* 149). In *Perchance to Dream*, the Sternwood and Simpson mansions, Marlowe's office, and the sanitarium Resthaven are located in the Los Angeles area. In *Love and Glory*, Boone Adams hits the skids and begins to pull himself together in Los Angeles.

Louisville, KY. Sunny Randall accompanies author Melanie Joan Hall on book tour here in *Shrink Rap*.

Lowell, MA. Working-class suburb of Boston where Congressman Meade Alexander campaigns in *The Widening Gyre*.

Lynnfield, MA. Where Sigmund "Ziggy" Czernak and his wife live, in *Back Story*.

Manchester, MA. Where Trent and Marlene Rowley live, in *Bad Business*.

Marblehead, MA. Where Luis Deleon lives, in *Thin Air*. It's also the location of the house in which Richie Burke and Sunny Randall lived when they were married in *Family Honor*. In *Love and Glory*, Marblehead is Jennifer Grayle's hometown.

Marblehead Neck, MA. Well-off Boston suburb on the Atlantic Ocean where Francis Ronan lives in *Sudden Mischief*. In *Love and Glory*, it is the home of Jennifer and John Merchent.

Marlborough Street (Boston). The site of Spenser's apartment.

Marshport, MA. The town where Boots Podolak is mayor, in *Cold Service*. The four Ukrainian mobsters Hawk is seeking also live here.

Massachusetts Avenue Bridge (Boston). Spenser sets up an exchange between the feuding Giacomins on the bridge in *Early Autumn*.

Mazza Mall. Tony shopping center in northwest Washington, D.C., which Susan and Spenser visit in *The Widening Gyre*. It is more properly called the Mazza Gallerie and is described by Spenser as "Rodeo Drive compressed" (*The Widening Gyre* 141).

Middlesex Fells Reservation. Thick woods where two thugs attempt to get the drop on Sunny Randall in *Melancholy Baby*.

Middleton, MA. The site of the founding church of the Reorganized Church of the Redemption in *Valediction*. Spenser stops off for a cup of coffee in the Blue Bell Restaurant. The church has substations in Wilmington, Lakeville, and West Boylston.

Mill River, CA. A suburb south of San Francisco that is home to arms dealer Jerry Costigan (*A Catskill Eagle*) and the jail where Hawk is locked up.

Milton, MA. An upper-middle-class suburb south of Boston; location of the Blue Hills Observatory, where Jane and Rose Alexander meet with Pam Shepard and Spenser to discuss a gun buy in *Promised Land*. In *Widow's Walk*, Spenser and Felton Shawcross have a shootout in Milton.

Moline, IL. Location of talk radio station WMOL in *Melancholy Baby*.

Montecito, CA. In *Small Vices*, where Spenser spends time with Susan Silverman and Hawk, convalescing from a serious gunshot wound.

Montreal, Quebec, Canada. Spenser and Hawk track their quarry to the final destination, Montreal, site of the Olympic Games, in *The Judas Goat*. Important scenes occur at the Olympic Stadium and its environs.

Natick, MA. Location of the Locksley Hall Motel in *Perish Twice*.

Neville Valley, CA. Some two hundred miles north of Los Angeles, Neville Valley is the center of Randolph Simpson's plans in *Perchance to Dream*.

New Bedford, MA (southeastern Massachusetts). In *Promised Land*, Pam Shepard takes refuge from her husband in New Bedford, forty-five miles from her home in Hyannis, and Spenser consults with New Bedford detectives to set up loanshark King Powers. Spenser likens it to "newsreel footage of the Warsaw ghetto" (*Promised Land* 48). New Bedford is Boone Adams's hometown in *Love and Glory*.

Newburyport, MA. Susan goes shopping here in *Widow's Walk*.

New York City. Spenser looks for information on Linda Rabb's past, visiting the Department of Social Services and a rundown apartment building in the East Village, among other places, in *Mortal Stakes*. He goes to Midtown East Side Manhattan to call on Patricia Utley. He dines with her at a restaurant called The Wings of the Dove on Sixty-fifth Street. In *Early Autumn* Spenser travels to New York with Susan Silverman and Paul Giacomin to track down some information on Patty Giacomin's activities. In *Taming a Sea-Horse* Spenser dines with Patricia Utley at a restaurant called Bogie's on Manhattan's West Side. Utley tells Spenser that April Kyle has once again disappeared. Spenser meets April at the Brasserie, right under the Four Seasons. In *Small Vices* Spenser visits with Clint Stapleton's parents to talk about the Melissa Henderson case. Spenser also goes to see Patricia Utley later in the book; she has now moved uptown to Sixty-fifth Street, between Park and Madison Avenues. In *Shrink Rap,* Sunny Randall and Melanie Joan Hall go here to talk to film producer Murray Gottlieb and actor Hal Race at the Hotel Carlyle. In *Melancholy Baby,* Randall confronts disbarred lawyer Ike Rosen at his apartment on West Ninety-second Street. Also in *Melancholy Baby*, Randall meets attorney Peter Franklin at his office near Carnegie Hall and has a drink with him at the Four Seasons Grill Room. She also goes to the Hotel Saint Regis to discuss Franklin's murder with New York detective second-grade Eugene Corsetti, and she and Corsetti visit July Fishbein at her townhouse in the West Village. In *Love and Glory*, Boone Adams gets a job in an insurance firm in New York City after his army discharge. In *Double Play*, Julius Roach's apartment is located on

Fifth Avenue at Eighty-first Street, and Joseph Burke and Lauren Roach go to the Waldorf Hotel. Also in *Double Play*, Burke and Lauren make love in Central Park, and the Dodgers play the Giants at the Polo Grounds. Burke meets gangster Johnny Paglia at a bar called Freddy's on Eighth Avenue.

Newton, MA. Where Clint Stapleton has a condo, in *Small Vices*. KC Roth's former husband, Burton Roth, lives here with their daughter, in *Hush Money*.

North End (Boston). Location of Marvin Conroy's apartment in *Widow's Walk*.

Paradise, MA. In *Back Story* this is where Sonny Karnofsky lives. Spenser and Hawk meet Jesse Stone here while they're on a stakeout.

Park Square (Boston). Where Sunny Randall goes looking for the missing Millicent Patton in *Family Honor*; also the location of Mary Lou Goddard's office in *Perish Twice*.

Park Street Station (Boston). In the opening scene of *Stardust*, Spenser and Susan Silverman are approaching this subway station, where filming is taking place for an episode of the show *Fifty Minutes*.

Peabody, MA. Site of the Northshore Shopping Center and where Spenser and Jeanette Ronan meet in *Sudden Mischief*. "It was someplace to go for young mothers with unhappy children, and old people on whom the walls had begun to close" (*Sudden Mischief* 185).

Pemberton College. In *Small Vices* the fictional Massachusetts school attended by murder victim Melissa Henderson. She was allegedly abducted from the campus by Ellis Alves, and Spenser visits the campus several times in his search for information.

Pequod. A fictitious town west of Hartford, CT, on the Farmington River, it is the location of Jerry Costigan's mercenary camp in *A Catskill Eagle*. Because the title of *A Catskill Eagle* is taken from Herman Melville's *Moby Dick*, Parker is probably referring to Ahab's ship the *Pequod* in his name for the town.

Philadelphia, PA. In *Double Play*, the Brooklyn Dodgers play the Phillies here, and a black cat is tossed out onto the field during the game (as a derogatory action against Jackie Robinson).

Pittsburgh, PA. In *Double Play*, Jackie Robinson meets with a group of men in Pittsburgh who offer a lucrative deal for him to play in the Negro leagues.

Pittsfield, MA. In *Pastime* Spenser spends a little time in a hospital here, after an adventure in the woods along the Massachusetts Turnpike.

Pleasure Bay, MA. Conn Sheridan takes his son Gus here to fish in *All Our Yesterdays*.

Plum Island. Spenser and Susan go for a walk on the beach here in *Widow's Walk*.

Plimoth Plantation (Plymouth, MA). In *Promised Land*, Spenser meets a hunted Pam Shepard at the reconstructed Plimoth Plantation, where Spenser says he experiences "a sense of the desolation" of the Pilgrims (*Promised Land* 101).

Pomona, CA. Spenser and Susan Silverman stop here at the Pomona State Hospital in *Thin Air* during their quest for information on the background of Lisa St. Claire.

Poodle Springs, CA. Desert town of the wealthy where the newly married Philip and Linda Marlowe reside in *Poodle Springs*, which may be a thinly disguised Palm Springs.

Port City. Port City is a fictional former mill town and current fishing port with a cross-section of residents from WASP, Chinese, and Portuguese backgrounds. It hosts the Port City Theater, site of the first murder in *Walking Shadow*.

Portland, ME. Spenser's quest for information on Ginger Buckey leads him here, in *Taming a Sea-Horse*.

Potshot, AZ. Town in the Arizona desert under the thumb of a gang in *Potshot*.

Proctor, MA. Town near the New Hampshire border; site of the radio station where Lisa St. Claire works and also of Merrimack College, where Lisa has been taking some classes, in *Thin Air*. This is also the town where Luis Deleon is trying to build his own little crime empire, despite opposition from Freddie Santiago.

Providence, RI. In *Ceremony* Spenser travels here looking for April Kyle.

Queens, NY. Joseph Burke and Jackie Robinson attend a birthday party in the Queens neighborhood of St. Albans in *Double Play*.

Quincy, MA. Where the Paultz Construction Company is located, in *Valediction*.

Quincy Market (Boston). Boston tourist attraction with a large food market, cafes, and shops. In *Looking for Rachel Wallace*, Spenser and Susan eat oysters and fruit there. In *Sudden Mischief*, Spenser meets

Richard Gavin for lunch at Quincy Market. In *Family Honor*, Spike's restaurant Beans & Rice is located near here.

Rancho Springs, CA. Some thirty miles east of Pasadena, the desert Rancho Springs is a key component of Randolph Simpson's plans in *Perchance to Dream*.

Reading, MA. Spenser visits Susan Silverman's friend, KC Roth, at her apartment here in *Hush Money* to discuss her case.

Redford, IL. Small town where Spenser goes, seeking information on Linda Rabb's background, in *Mortal Stakes*.

Riverside, CA. Location of the casino the Agony Club in *Poodle Springs*.

Rowes Wharf (Boston). Condos that are part of a big waterfront complex; Brock and Jolene Rimbaud live here in *Cold Service*. In *Double Deuce*, Susan and Spenser have dinner here in the Boston Harbor Hotel.

Roxbury, MA. Site of the "spiffy new police headquarters" on Tremont Street in *Hush Money* where Spenser talks with Belson in his "spiffy new cubicle" (*Hush Money* 19). It's also where Sunny Randall meets vice cop Bobby Franco for coffee in *Perish Twice*.

St. Louis, MO. The Dodgers play the Cardinals here in *Double Play*, and Jackie Robinson is spiked at first base.

Saint Thomas, U.S. Virgin Islands. In *Taming a Sea-Horse* Spenser and Susan head here, so that Spenser can dig up information on the Crown Prince Club, Ginger Buckey, and April Kyle.

Salem, MA. Where Spenser goes to find Art Floyd, in *Taming a Sea-Horse*.

Salisbury, MA. Site of a substation of the Reorganized Church of the Redemption, where Spenser goes to visit Sherry Spellman in *Valediction*.

San Diego, CA. Spenser travels west in *Stardust*, seeking information on Jill Joyce's past. In *Back Story* Spenser goes back to find Barry Gordon, Daryl Silver's father; he has a house in Mission Bay.

San Francisco, CA. Hawk and Spenser hide out in an apartment in the Mission District after their jailbreak in *A Catskill Eagle*. In *Hugger Mugger*, Spenser and Susan travel to San Francisco to speak to Sherry Lark. "In the distance, the Bay was everywhere, creating the ambient luminescence of an impressionist painting" (*Hugger Mugger* 214).

Santa Monica, CA. Spenser goes here to investigate the past of Mary Lou and Steve Buckman in *Potshot*.

Saratoga, NY. The noted New York horseracing venue is the setting for Hugger Mugger's race in the Hopeful in *Hugger Mugger*.

Shaker Heights, OH. Location of the Regal Bookstore in *Shrink Rap*.

Smithfield, MA. A suburb north of Boston, where the parents of April Kyle live, in *Ceremony*, and where Susan Silverman is working as guidance counselor at a high school. It's also home to Kevin Bartlett, the kidnapped child in *God Save the Child*. Aaron and Janet Newman, the main characters of *Wilderness*, live here, and it's where Aaron witnesses a murder.

Somerville, MA. Boston suburb on the Mystic River where the late Prentice Lamont's mother lives, in *Hush Money*. It's also the site of the Pulaski Social Club, where Sonny Karnofsky runs his business in *Back Story*. Civil Streets president Carla Quagliotti lives here in *Sudden Mis-*

chief. In *All Our Yesterdays* Gus Sheridan has a private meeting with Pat Malloy outside a Dunkin' Donuts shop in Union Square.

South Bay (Boston). Location of the Suffolk County House of Correction in *Widow's Walk*.

South Boston, MA. Location of Race Witherspoon's studio and Jack DeRosa's apartment in *Widow's Walk*. In *Family Honor* and *Perish Twice*, Sunny Randall lives in a Fort Point loft near the waterfront and Brian Kelly has a brick townhouse in South Boston. Also in *Perish Twice*, Sunny and Julie have lunch in the Boston Harbor Hotel. In *Shrink Rap*, Richie Burke's condo is located here on a Commercial Street wharf.

The South End (Boston). Area of Boston where Spenser and Hawk go in search of April Kyle in *Ceremony*. Spenser and Hawk meet Tony Marcus in his regular South End hangout, Buddy's Fox, in *Sudden Mischief*. Sunny Randall also goes to Buddy's Fox in *Family Honor* and *Perish Twice*. In *Widow's Walk*, the South End is the location of Larson Graff's home and business. In *Family Honor*, Sunny Randall looks for Millicent Patton among the prostitutes in the South End, and Spike's townhouse is located here. In *All Our Yesterdays* Mellen Murphy lives here on K Street, and when she and Conn Sheridan marry they set up house here. It's also home to the feuding Irish gangs, the O'Briens and the Malloys.

South Natick, MA. Location of Brock and Betty Patton's mansion in *Family Honor*.

Springfield, MA. City in western Massachusetts near Amherst where two young campaign workers for Meade Alexander get roughed up by the opposition in *The Widening Gyre*. It also is the hometown of the character Bobby in *Double Play*.

Stockbridge, MA. One of the towns in *Pastime* where Spenser and Paul Giacomin go looking for the missing Patty Giacomin.

Stoneham, MA. Location of Gretchen Crane's apartment in *Perish Twice*.

Stuart Street (Boston). Site of Spenser's office in early books.

Sudbury, MA. Where Anne Fahey lives, in *Back Story*.

Swampscott, MA. Site, opposite King's Beach, of Mrs. Felton's house in *Crimson Joy*. Location of Cathal Kragan's house in *Family Honor*.

Tacoma, WA. In an effort to locate Susan, Spenser and Hawk drive to Crystal Mountain in Tacoma to a lodge owned by arms dealer Jerry Costigan (*A Catskill Eagle*). In *Love and Glory*, Boone Adams works here picking cranberries.

Taft University (Walford, MA). In *Small Vices* Spenser visits the campus to speak to tennis star Clint Stapleton about the Melissa Henderson case. In *Back Story* Spenser and Hawk have a deadly confrontation here while looking for information in the Emily Gordon case.

Tokyo, Japan. While in the army, Boone Adams and Tony dePietro go here on R&R in *Love and Glory*.

Tombstone, AZ. Tombstone and the surrounding area are the setting for most of the action in *Gunman's Rhapsody*.

Venice Beach, CA. In *Thin Air*, this is yet another stop in Spenser and Susan Silverman's search for information on the background of Lisa St. Claire. It's also home of bigamist photographer Larry Victor in *Poodle Springs*.

Walford, MA. Town west of Boston that is the home of Taft University (*Playmates; Love and Glory; Small Vices; Back Story*).

Waltham, MA. Site of the offices of the energy trading firm, Kinergy, in *Bad Business*. Location of Mort Kraken's warehouse in *Perish Twice*.

Waymark, MA. West of Boston in the Berkshire Hills, this is the town where Wilfred Pomeroy lives, in *Stardust*.

Wellesley, MA. Location of the office of Millicent Patton's therapist in *Family Honor*. In *Perish Twice*, Spike, Sunny Randall, Elizabeth Reagan, and Mort Krakan eat at the Blue Ginger restaurant in Wellesley.

West Concord, MA. Location of Kim Crawford's condo in *Shrink Rap*.

West Newton, MA. A tony Boston suburb where Terry Orchard and her parents live in *The Godwulf Manuscript*.

Weston, MA. Boston suburb where Hugh Dixon lives in *The Judas Goat*. Sunny Randall's sister lives here in *Perish Twice*, and it's also where her husband's girlfriend lives. In *All Our Yesterdays* Thomas Winslow, Sr., owns a house here, one used for unpleasant purposes by his son, Thomas Jr.

Wheaton, MA. A town about a hundred miles west of Boston with connections to Colombia, Wheaton is identified as a major center of cocaine traffic in the Northeast in *Pale Kings and Princes*.

Williamstown, MA. In *Paper Doll* Spenser travels to Williams College to talk to the Tripp children about their murdered mother, Olivia Nelson.

Worcester, MA. Ann Kiley checks into a hotel in Worcester in *Widow's Walk*.

NOTABLE QUOTATIONS

S penser has a quick wit, which has provided some memorable dialogue throughout the books. And the discussions he sometimes has
with Susan about his life, their relationship, and his job can be very
illuminating. Here is a very select group of quotations from the books.

"I don't know if there is even a name for the system I've chosen,
but it has to do with honor. And honor is behavior for its own reason . . . Whatever the hell I am is based in part on not doing things
I don't think I should do. Or don't want to do." (*Mortal Stakes*)

"Then [Susan] said, 'It's where you lose me, this arcane male thing.
It's like a set of rituals from a religion that no longer exists, the rules
of a kingdom that disappeared before memory. It can't be questioned
or explained, it simply is—like gravity or inertia.' " (*Ceremony*)

"The world is full of people I can't save. I get used to that. I got
used to it on the cops. Any cop does. You have to or you go down
the tube too." (*Early Autumn*)

Susan, talking about her relationship with Spenser, when he talks about having killed people: "It makes no difference to them why you did it. But it makes a difference to me and to you. What we've been through in the last couple of years has produced the relationship we have now, achieved love, maybe. Something we've earned, something we've paid for in effort and pain and maybe mistakes as well. I live with some." (*Taming a Sea-Horse*)

Susan, talking about Spenser and violence: "We all do what we need to, and what we have to, not what we ought to, or ought to have. You're a violent man. You wouldn't do your work if you weren't. What makes you so attractive, among other things, is that your capacity for violence is never random, it is rarely self-indulgent, and you don't take it lightly. You make mistakes. But they are mistakes of judgment. They are not mistakes of the heart." (*Taming a Sea-Horse*)

Spenser, talking about his feelings for Susan: "It is not only that I love you. It is that you complete my every shortfall." And a little further on: "And I complete yours. Our strengths and weaknesses interlock so perfectly that together we are more than the sum of our parts." (*Crimson Joy*)

Susan, talking about Spenser: "Except maybe for Hawk, you look at the world with fewer illusions than anyone I have ever known. And yet you are as sentimental as you would be if the world were pretty-pretty." (*Pastime*)

Spenser, reflecting on his work and why he does it: "Several people had died so far in pursuit of information that no one might wish to acquire. They hadn't been good people. But I had known I'd have to kill them when I led them to the stadium, where I knew the layout and they didn't. I hadn't known there'd be backup. But

I hadn't known there wouldn't be. Did I stick at it because I was curious? Because I was a nosy guy who wanted to know what everyone had been covering up? Now I knew. Or at least I knew most of it. Was it worth a lot of dead guys? I did this work because I could. And maybe because I couldn't do any other. I'd never been good at working for someone. At least this work let me live life on my terms." (*Back Story*)

Spenser, attempting to explain Hawk to Cecile: "He doesn't want to [change]. That's the center of him. He is what he wants to be. It's how he's handled the world." (*Cold Service*)

Referring to Mark Tabor, political counselor of SCACE: "He looked like a zinnia." (*The Godwulf Manuscript*)

"It was good not to be dead in the mud under a blue spruce tree." (*The Godwulf Manuscript*)

"The office of the university president looked like the front parlor of a successful Victorian whorehouse." (*The Godwulf Manuscript*)

"They were domestic adversaries again, tripping the same old grim fantastic over the same old painful ground." ("Surrogate")

" 'You're almost perfect, you are, a flawless moron.' " (*The Godwulf Manuscript*)

" 'Your own life is always close up. You only see other people's lives at long range.' " (*The Godwulf Manuscript*)

"Should I unbutton the shirt two more buttons and wear a bullet around my neck on a gold chain? Too pushy. They might think I was an agent." (*A Savage Place*)

"Lots of real creeps have self-respect. They just have a creepy version of it." (*A Savage Place*)

"I turned on the TV and watched the early news and wondered why the early-news people in every city were wimps. Probably specified in the recruitment ads. *Early-News Person Wanted. Must Be Wimp.*" (*The Widening Gyre*)

Hawk: "I come out here to whack a couple of dope pushers and I end up in encounter therapy." (*Pale Kings and Princes*)

Leonard O: "Murder is the bloodiest of the creative arts." (*Walking Shadow*)

"I was neat and polite and generally swell, for a gumshoe." (*Walking Shadow*)

"*If a detective falls in the forest*, I thought, *does he make a sound?*" (*Walking Shadow*)

" 'So many assholes,' [Hawk] said. 'So little time.' " (*Sudden Mischief*)

"The donuts [sic] were everything donuts should be, and the bright beginning of the day contained the prospect of unlimited possibility." (*Hugger Mugger*)

" 'They could have tailed me with a walrus,' I said, 'and been better off.' " (*Hugger Mugger*)

"[. . .] I remained dashing and ineffable." (*Widow's Walk*)

Sunny Randall: "She was wearing one of those hideous print prairie dresses that are equally attractive on girls, women, and cattle." (*Family Honor*)

Marlowe: "The office was as blank as a waiter's stare." (*Poodle Springs*)

Marlowe: "On both sides of Sunset were big homes, expensive and ugly in that special way that Southern California money finds to combine both. Movie stars, directors, producers, agents, people who had found a way to package emptiness and sell it as dreams." (*Poodle Springs*)

Linda Marlowe: "What is a realtor?"
Marlowe: "A real estate man with a carnation." (*Poodle Springs*)

A ROBERT B. PARKER
BIBLIOGRAPHY

The Spenser Novels

The Godwulf Manuscript. Boston: Houghton Mifflin, 1974.

God Save the Child. Boston: Houghton Mifflin, 1974.

Mortal Stakes. Boston: Houghton Mifflin, 1975.

Promised Land. Boston: Houghton Mifflin, 1976.

The Judas Goat. Boston: Houghton Mifflin, 1978.

Looking for Rachel Wallace. New York: Delacorte, 1980.

Early Autumn. New York: Delacorte, 1981.

A Savage Place. New York: Delacorte, 1981.

Ceremony. New York: Delacorte, 1982.

The Widening Gyre. New York: Delacorte, 1983.

Valediction. New York: Delacorte, 1984.

A Catskill Eagle. New York: Delacorte, 1985.

Taming a Sea Horse. New York: Delacorte, 1986.

Pale Kings and Princes. New York: Delacorte, 1987.

Crimson Joy. New York: Delacorte, 1988.

Playmates. New York: Putnam, 1989.

Stardust. New York: Putnam, 1990.

Pastime. New York: Putnam, 1991.

Double Deuce. New York: Putnam, 1992.

Paper Doll. New York: Putnam, 1993.

Walking Shadow. New York: Putnam, 1994.

Thin Air. New York: Putnam, 1995.

Chance. New York: Putnam, 1996.

Small Vices. New York: Putnam, 1997.

Sudden Mischief. New York: Putnam, 1998.

Hush Money. New York: Putnam, 1999.

Hugger Mugger. New York: Putnam, 2000.

Potshot. New York: Putnam, 2001.

Widow's Walk. New York: Putnam, 2002.

Back Story. New York: Putnam, 2003.

Bad Business. New York: Putnam, 2004.

Cold Service. New York: Putnam, 2005.

The Sunny Randall Novels

Family Honor. New York: Putnam, 1999.

Perish Twice. New York: Putnam, 2000.

Shrink Rap. New York: Putnam, 2002.

Melancholy Baby. New York: Putnam, 2004.

The Jesse Stone Novels

Night Passage. New York: Putnam, 1997.

Trouble in Paradise. New York: Putnam, 1998.

Death in Paradise. New York: Putnam, 2001.

Stone Cold. New York: Putnam, 2003.

The Nonseries Novels

Wilderness. New York: Delacorte, 1979.

Love and Glory. New York: Delacorte, 1983.

Poodle Springs with Raymond Chandler. New York: Putnam, 1989.

Perchance to Dream. New York: Putnam, 1991.

All Our Yesterdays. New York: Delacorte, 1994.

Gunman's Rhapsody. New York: Putnam, 2001.

Double Play. New York: Putnam, 2004.

Appaloosa. New York: Putnam, 2005.

Articles

"The Big Text." *New York Times Book Review* vol. 145, issue 50208 (8 October 1995: p 22, 1p, 1bw. [Discusses the books *Raymond Chandler: Stories and Early Novels* and *Raymond Chandler: Later Novels and Other Writings* from the Library of America. Background on Chandler's literary career; Chandler's representation of Los Angeles; Characterization of Philip Marlowe; Value of biographer Frank MacShane's notes to the collection.]

"Creating a Series Character." *Writer* 94.1 (Jan 1981): 15–17.

"More Than a 'Mystery Writer.' " [Tribute to the late George V. Higgins] *Wall Street Journal* Eastern Edition vol. 234, issue 94 (11 November 1999): pA26, 0p, 1bw.

"Spenser Meets Sue Grafton." *Mystery Scene* 72 (2001): 31–32. [Tribute to Sue Grafton]

"What I Know about Writing Spenser Novels." *Colloquium on Crime: Eleven Renowned Mystery Writers Discuss Their Work*. Robin W. Winks, ed. New York: Scribners, 1986, 189–203. (Revised version of Ponder 1984)

Introductions

Introduction. *The Best American Mystery Stories 1997*. Robert B. Parker and Otto Penzler, eds. Boston: Houghton Mifflin, 1997.

Introduction. *Woman in the Dark: A Novel of Dangerous Romance*. By Dashiell Hammett. New York: Knopf, 1988.

Short Stories

"Harlem Nocturne." *Murderers' Row*. Otto Penzler, ed. New Millennium Press, 2001. [Reprinted in *The Best American Mystery Stories 2002*. James Ellroy, ed. Boston: Houghton Mifflin, 2002.]

"Surrogate." Northridge, CA: Lord John Press, 1982. (Story published as chapbook) [Reprinted in *New Crimes 3*. Maxim Jakubowski, ed. London: Robinson, 1991.]

Speeches

Luncheon Address. Friends of Libraries USA, ALA 105th Annual Conference, New York, 1986. Audiotape. Elkridge, MD: Chesapeake Audio/Video Communications.

Nonfiction

Boston: History in the Making. Urban Tapestry Ser. Memphis: Towery Publ., 1999.

Parker on Writing. Northridge, CA: Lord John Press, 1985.

The Private Eye in Chandler and Hammett. Northridge, CA: Lord John Press, 1984. (Version of "The Violent Hero, Wilderness Heritage, and Urban Reality: A Study of the Private Eye in the Novels of Dashiell Hammett, Raymond Chandler, and Ross Macdonald." Ph.D. Diss., Boston University, 1970.)

Spenser's Boston. New York: Otto Penzler Books, 1994.

(with John R. Marsh) *Sports Illustrated Training with Weights*. Lippincott, 1974.

(with Joan H. Parker) *Three Weeks in Spring*. Boston: Houghton Mifflin, 1978.

(with Joan H. Parker) *A Year at the Races*. New York: Viking, 1990.

The Personal Response to Literature. Robert B. Parker, ed. Boston: Houghton Mifflin, 1971.

Order and Diversity: The Craft of Prose. Robert B. Parker, and Peter L. Sandberg, eds. New York: Wiley, 1973.

Works about Robert B. Parker

Anthun, Morten. *Modern Masculinity: Robert B. Parker's Spenser Novels in the Context of the Mythopoetic Men's Movement*. M.A. thesis, Bowling Green State University, 1996.

Carter, Steven R. "Spenserian Ethics: The Unconventional Morality of Robert B. Parker's Traditional American Hero." *Clues: A Journal of Detection* 1.2 (Fall–Winter 1980): 109–18.

Casella, Donna R. "The Trouble with Susan: Women in Robert B. Parker's Spenser Novels." *Clues: A Journal of Detection* 10.2 (Fall–Winter 1989): 93–105.

Corrigan, Maureen. "Robert B. Parker." *Mystery and Suspense Writers: The Literature of Crime, Detection, and Espionage, I–II*. Robin W. Winks and Maureen Corrigan, eds. New York: Scribners, 1998, 715–32.

DeAndrea, William. "Parker, Robert B." *Encyclopedia Mysteriosa*. New York: Prentice Hall, 1994, 270.

Donnelly, Barry. "A Catcher in the Rye: Robert B. Parker's P.I. Spenser." *The Armchair Detective* 23.1 (Winter 1990): 12–25.

Eisman, Gregory D. "The Catskill Eagle Crashed: The Moral Demise of Spenser in Robert B. Parker's *A Catskill Eagle*." *Clues: A Journal of Detection* 11.1 (Spring–Summer 1990): 107–17.

Fackler, Herbert V. "Dialectic in the Corpus of Robert B. Parker's Spenser Novels." *Clues: A Journal of Detection* 16.1 (Spring–Summer 1995): 13–24.

———. "Spenser's New England Conscience." *Colby Quarterly* 34.3 (1988): 253–60.

Geherin, David. "Parker, Robert B." *The Oxford Companion to Crime & Mystery Writing*. Rosemary Herbert, ed. New York: Oxford UP, 1999, 325.

———. *Sons of Sam Spade: The Private-Eye Novel in the 70s: Robert B. Parker, Roger L. Simon, Andrew Bergman*. New York: Ungar, 1980.

Gorman, Ed. "A Few Minutes with Robert B. Parker." *Mystery Scene* 67 (2000): 23.

Gray, W. Russel. "Reflections in a Private Eye: Robert B. Parker's Spenser." *Clues: A Journal of Detection* 5.1 (Spring–Summer 1984): 1–13.

Greiner, Donald J., "Robert B. Parker and the Jock of the Mean Streets." *Critique* 26 (1984): 36–44.

Harper, Donna Waller. *The Image of Women in Robert B. Parker's Spenser Novels*. Ph.D. Diss., Middle Tennessee State University, 1993. [Diss Abstracts Intl: 1993 Aug; 54 (2): 514A.]

Hoffman, Carl. "Spenser: The Illusion of Knighthood." *The Armchair Detective* 16.2 (Spring 1983): 131–43.

Judas Goats. *The Godwulf Manuscript: The Journal of the Judas Goats, An Association of Parker/Spenser Devotees*. Semiannual periodical (twice a year). Cambridge, MA: Author, 1980s?

Kifner, John. "He Said He Had a Pistol; Then He Flashed a Knife." [Profile of author Robert B. Parker]. *New York Times* vol. 146, issue 50820 (11 June 1997) pC1, 2bw.

Kisor, Henry. "Parker's Still An Ace, But Is He Flying on Autopilot?" *Chicago Sun-Times* (14 March 2004) 14.

Kurata, Marilyn J. "Robert B. Parker: An Interview." *Clues: A Journal of Detection* 12.1 (Spring–Summer 1991): 1–31.

"The Many Faces of Robert B. Parker." *Book* (September–October 2002): 21.

Mason, Anthony. "Fine Print: Robert B. Parker." *CBS Sunday Morning*. CBS, New York. 12 March 2000.

"Mass Murder: Juggling Three Book Series, Including a New Spenser Novel, Robert B. Parker Is Boston's Peerless Man of Mystery." *Entertainment Weekly* (31 March 2000) 62.

McFarlane, Clive. "Parker Brings Spenser to the City." *Worcester [MA] Telegram & Gazette* (1 April 2004) C3.

McGee, Celia. "He's the Old Ball Parker." *Daily News* (31 May 2004) 30.

Nickell, Kelly. "Robert B. Parker's Boston." *Writer's Digest* 80.10 (2000): 16.

Older, Jules. "Private I." [Interview with Robert B. Parker]. *Yankee* 67.8 (October 2003): 72.

Parks, Louis B. "Mystery Men; Comparisons Natural between Parker and Fictional Spenser." *Houston Chronicle* (21 December 2003) 18.

Penzler, Otto. "Robert B. Parker." *Armchair Detective* 18.3 (Summer 1985): 258–61. (On collecting Parker)

Ponder, Anne. "A Dialogue with Robert B. Parker." *Armchair Detective* 17.4 (Fall 1984): 340–48.

Presley, John W. "Theory into Practice: Robert Parker's Re-Interpretation of the American Tradition." *Journal of American Culture* 12.3 (Fall 1989): 27–30.

Prinster, Thomas. *The Evolution of a Hero: The Spenser Novels of Robert Parker*. M.A. thesis, University of Rhode Island, 1991.

Ranalli, Ralph. "Once Upon Crime." *Boston Globe Magazine* (15 August 2004) 18–27. [Boston as setting for mystery novels, including quotes from Parker on his views.]

"Robert B. Parker." *Contemporary Literary Criticism*. Vol. 27. Detroit: Gale, 1984.

"Robert B(rown) Parker." *Contemporary Authors* Online. Detroit: Gale, 2004.

Robinson, Doug. *No Less a Man: Masculist Art in a Feminist Age*. Bowling Green, OH: Popular Press, 1994. (Treatment of Spenser as hero)

Root, Christina. "Silence of the Other: Women in Robert Parker's Spenser Series." *Clues: A Journal of Detection* 19.1 (1988): 25–38.

Saylor, V. Louise. "The Private Eye and His Victuals." *Clues: A Journal of Detection* 5.2 (Fall–Winter 1984): 111–18. (Treatment of food; of private eye)

Schaefer, Eric, and Eithne Johnson. "Quarantine! A Case Study of Boston's Combat Zone." *Hop on Pop: The Politics and Pleasures of Popular Culture*. Henry Jenkins, Tara McPherson, and Jane Shattuc, eds. Durham, NC: Duke UP; 2002, 430–53. (Treatment of Red Light districts in film)

Sheehan, Nancy. " 'Spenser' Fare; Robert B. Parker Offers Insight into Genesis of Prolific, Terrific Fiction." *Worcester [MA] Telegram & Gazette* (28 Mar 2003) C1.

Svoboda, Frederic. "Hard-Boiled Feminist Detectives and Their Families: Reimaging a Form." *Gender in Popular Culture: Images of Men and Women in Literature, Visual Media, and Material Culture*. Jane S. Bakerman, ed. Cleveland: Ridgemont, 1995, 247–72.

Tallett, Dennis. *The Spenser Companion: The Godwulf Manuscript to Hugger Mugger: A Reader's Guide*. CA: Companion Books, 2001.

————. *The Spenser Companion: The "Godwulf Manuscript" to "Small Vices," A Reader's Guide*. CA: Companion Bks, 1997.

Thompson, George J. "Parker, Robert B." *Twentieth-Century Crime and Mystery Writers*. John M. Reilly, ed. 2nd ed. New York: St. Martin's, 1985, 695–97.

West, J. Alec. "An Interview with Robert B. Parker." *Murderous Intent* 5.1 (Spring 1999): 4.

Whitehead, Gwendolyn. *The Hard-Boiled Heir: Robert B. Parker as Literary Descendant of Dashiell Hammett, Raymond Chandler, and Ross MacDonald*. Ph.D. Diss., University of Southwestern Louisiana, 1992. [Diss Abstracts Intl, 1992 Dec; 53 (6): 1919A.]

Willis, Lonnie. "Henry David Thoreau and the Hard Boiled Dick." *Thoreau Society Bulletin* 170 (Winter 1985): 1–3.

Zaleski, Jeff. "Interview with Robert B. Parker." *Publishers Weekly* (8 October 2001) 46.

Zalewski, James W., and Lawrence B. Rosenfield. "Rules for the Game of Life: The Mysteries of Robert B. Parker and Dick Francis." *Clues: A Journal of Detection* 5.2 (Fall–Winter 1984): 72–81.

Zivley, Sherry Lutz. "Hemingway's 'Pretty' Illusions in American Fiction." *Notes on Contemporary Literature* 22.1 (Jan 1992): 11–12. (Hemingway's influence on Parker)

Web Sites and Internet Groups

Book Reporter.com. http://www.bookreporter.com/authors/au-parker-robert.asp

Bullets and Beer. http://bullets-and-beer.com

Cluelass. http://www.cluelass.com

DorothyL. http://www.dorothyl.com

Mystery Ink page on Parker. http://www.mysteryinkonline.com/rbparker.htm

Robert B. Parker. http://www.booksnbytes.com/authors/parker_robertb.html

Robert Brown Parker. http://hycyber.com/MYST/parker_robert_b.html

The Spensarium. http://www.spensarium.com. A division of the Spensarium Web site is the discussion group on Spenser: http://tv.groups.yahoo.com/group/spenser

Spenser's Sneakers. Another discussion group on Parker's works: http://groups.yahoo.com/group/spensneak

The Thrilling Detective's Spenser page. http://www.thrillingdetective.com/spenser.html

Awards

Grand Master, Mystery Writers of America. 2002.

Mystery Writers of America Edgar Allan Poe Award for Best Novel: *Promised Land* (1977).

Edgar Nominee, Best Episode in a TV Series (*Blues for Buder*, 1990).

Private Eye Writers of America Shamus Award Nominee, Best PI Novel: *Early Autumn* (1982), *Ceremony* (1983), *The Widening Gyre* (1984), *A Catskill Eagle* (1986)

Dean James won an Agatha Award for *By a Woman's Hand: A Guide to Mystery Fiction by Women,* and is the author of several other works of mystery non-fiction. His novels include the Simon Kirby-Jones mystery series. He is the manager of Murder By the Book in Houston, Texas.

Elizabeth Foxwell is the editor of numerous mystery anthologies, including the serial novel *The Sunken Sailor.* Her own short stories have appeared in *The World's Finest Mystery and Crime Stories* and elsewhere. She is the managing editor of *CLUES: A Journal of Detection,* America's only academic publication focusing on crime fiction.